Faith Within Reason

D0912118

This page intentionally left blank

Faith Within Reason

Herbert McCabe OP

Edited and introduced by Brian Davies OP

continuum

Continuum 80 Maiden Lane
The Tower Building Suite 704
11 York Road New York
London SE1 7NX NY 10038

www.continuumbooks.com

© The Estate of Herbert McCabe OP 2007

All rights reserved. No part of this publication may be reproduced or transmitted in any form or by any means, electronic or mechanical, including photocopying, recording or any information storage or retrieval system, without prior permission from the publishers.

First published 2007

British Library Cataloguing-in-Publication Data
A catalogue record for this book is available from the British Library.

ISBN 0 8264 9547 8

Typeset by TechBooks, New Delhi, India
Printed and bound by
Athenaeum Press Ltd., Gateshead, Tyne & Wear

Contents

Foreword

Bearing in mind the current state of all too much theological writing, I sometimes advise students contemplating their semester papers above all to avoid writing just 'more stuff about stuff'. Herbert McCabe had an abhorrence of theological 'stuff' – that surplus production in theology which has much the same inflationary outcomes as in the economic, a vacuity of thought wrapped up in a theological tribal dialect, a *patois* doing poor duty for the absence of creative imagination. And he had a similarly healthy contempt for the sort of nonsense in which much theological writing can find itself entangled, usually, as he supposed, as a result of conceptual muddles about God. Much of the sheer energy of his own writing was motivated by a Wittgensteinian goal of conceptual therapy, sorely needed in a field in which, to be fair, the distinction between the sublime and the ridiculous is in the nature of the case unusually difficult to detect.

You did not expect always to agree with Herbert. Least of all did he expect it, whether in the pub, arguing with him, in the study, or reading a collection of his papers and sermons such as is contained in this further posthumous volume. And by the way, for all that Herbert genuinely believed that good theology was possible only as the outcome of good company – and friendship was his model for 'good company' – he could be on occasions quite frighteningly aggressive in argument. But never for a moment did he imagine that friendship could be threatened by the cut and thrust of debate, however hot it became. In fact he once said that what characterized 'Dominican' obedience was its commitment to settling community questions by means of what he called the 'palaver' of debate. And you nearly always knew what you disagreed with him about, for Herbert had perfected to an unparalleled degree – in my experience of theologians – that clarity of writing which is to the intellectual life what humility is to the moral: namely a vulnerability to counter-argument and contrary evidence. A horror of obfuscation meant that Herbert never wrote 'stuff' – which meant that you could always see for yourself when, if you so thought, he was writing nonsense.

Herbert published little in his lifetime. His style was not generally that of the extended monograph. And this is because Herbert was above all a teacher: oral communication was his preferred *métier*. Luckily, however, he never extemporized, and he would always write out in full even the briefest and most occasional sermon, and many of these texts have survived, even if Herbert himself was frequently careless of preserving them (his friend Enda McDonagh tells of how the first page of Herbert's celebrated lecture on the politics of John's gospel was eventually retrieved from his shoe where it was plugging a leaky sole). In all of them Herbert wrote as a teacher speaks, and those who ever heard him in person can still hear through the written word that faintly Northumbrian drawl, the throwaway (if contrived) casualness of his most challenging paradoxes, the abrupt shifts from extreme conceptual exactness to an equally exact but tellingly homely example. These were the conscious but never self-consciously 'arty' skills of a true rhetorician, of a Dominican preacher who enacted in his practice that love of language as the most distinctive of human characteristics, because it is in and through language that we make or break human communities. Herbert, the Dominican, above all wanted to *share* the treasures he found in Thomas Aquinas, Wittgenstein and, first and foremost, the gospels. *Contemplata aliis tradere* was no pat slogan for Herbert. It was his life, for as he used to say, 'Dominicans don't pray. They teach.'

Herbert was perhaps the cleverest man I ever met. And some of the essays in this new collection are distinctly 'clever' in the sense that they challenge the reader's brains with a subtlety in which theological minds are often, alas, unpractised. Not all readers will find the chapters on 'Evil and Omnipotence' and on 'Soul, Life, Machines and Language' as easy a read as are some others: clear as they are, their clarity is a challenge to our conceptually sloppier styles of doing theology. But if he acquired much of that skill in making dauntingly precise distinctions from his constant reading of Thomas Aquinas, he followed Thomas in this above all, that he thought of himself as engaged in a task which was really very simple: explaining the gospel. And perhaps it was something even simpler that he aimed for, for he always said that all he tried to do was to remind his audiences of what they could already know for themselves from the gospels, if only they could be got to clear their minds of a sort of semi-pagan, and idolatrous, understanding of God which had no place in them. Again and again, in these essays Herbert returns to that Augean task of clearing away philosophical and theological clutter, 'stuff'. And if that might seem an excessively negative way of characterizing his theological role, I recommend readers of this collection that they begin by reading his very brief, but intensely moving, sermon on 'Forgiveness' – the more moving because Herbert makes absolutely no 'homiletic' attempt to 'move' – and then consider how a man could preach that sermon who had not first settled conceptual accounts with the 'Free-Will Defence' in Chapter 6, or with the determinist materialists in Chapter 9. That goal, and that capacity, to liberate the gospels so as to speak for themselves has the effect of an ancient picture restored: there is a freshness to how things seem when Herbert has done with them, and that word 'freshness' is no bad translation of the Latin *claritas*, which, as Thomas says, is one of the chief characteristics of the beautiful.

I once asked Herbert (knowing his love of paradox) what he thought of Chesterton. He replied that Chesterton was his model of good theological writing. Josef Pieper, in what in my view is the best short introduction to the spirit of Thomas Aquinas's theology, says that in his view Chesterton's is the best short introduction to the spirit of Thomas Aquinas's theology. Not, in my view, is Herbert's 'A Very Short Introduction to Aquinas' (Chapter 7) the best contribution in this volume, since it tails off, somewhat perfunctorily incomplete. I think this is symptomatic of something important about Herbert's relationship to Thomas Aquinas. He was too close to Thomas – and too impatient of pedantry – to be a good detailed expositor of him. In any case Herbert was no 'Thomist' if a Thomist is someone who thinks *about* Thomas. He thought *with* Thomas, and Thomas came alive in Herbert's theology. Paradoxically, it is often just when Herbert is thinking most closely with Thomas that it is least easy to annotate his texts with accurate referencing to their 'source'. And therein lies another paradox. It is not just that Thomas comes alive in Herbert, but that through Thomas Herbert came alive. I think, in the end, this is what chiefly characterizes Herbert's sense of vocation, as theologian and as Dominican priest: that, for him, intellect, in its own nature as a simple human power but above all as a power to which God has disclosed something of his own self-understanding (which in us Herbert called 'faith'), is a way, and in the end the only way, of being alive. For it is only through that disclosure of God's inner life to our human minds that we can know of the one, primary truth from which all Herbert's theology derives, and to which it always returns, as every essay in this volume witnesses: not that we ought to love God but that we are able to do so because from eternity God has loved us first. And that is the only 'gospel' that Herbert ever preached.

Denys Turner
Yale University

Introduction

Though one of the most gifted thinkers of his generation, Herbert McCabe, who died in 2001, published relatively little in his lifetime. He did, however, leave behind a number of unpublished essays, talks and sermons, some of which have now appeared in three volumes: *God Still Matters* (Continuum, 2002), *God, Christ and Us* (Continuum, 2003), and *The Good Life* (Continuum, 2005). All of these books have been very favourably reviewed and I have therefore ransacked McCabe's remains so as to offer readers yet another collection by him. Those familiar with McCabe's writings, and appreciative of them, will not, I think, be disappointed with what follows, since it shows him at his best while concerned with what interested him most.

For many years now there has been a notable rift between philosophers and theologians. Typically, philosophers have not engaged with theologians (even in the rare cases when they have been sympathetic to them), and theologians have displayed little interest in (and often little competence for) detailed philosophical analysis. Things were quite different in the Middle Ages, when professors (or masters) of theology were normally very well read in philosophical texts and anxious to show the relevance of philosophy for what they maintained as religious believers. Aquinas is, perhaps, the classic example of such a professor. He formally lectured on biblical texts and wrote treatises on matters of Christian dogmatics. Yet he constantly seeks to argue on the basis of reason and to engage both with philosophical arguments and with philosophers as such.

Aquinas is the writer whom Herbert McCabe most admired. His influence on McCabe can be seen in almost everything

McCabe wrote. This includes the essays in the present work, many of which are therefore not easily classifiable as examples of philosophy, on the one hand, or theology, on the other. Perhaps they can be labelled 'philosophical theology'. At any rate, readers will find in them an attempt to marry the best we can think on our own with the content of divine revelation (McCabe always believed that truth could never contradict truth). Can we think of faith as reasonable? What is faith? How far can reason take us when it comes to things divine? Do we have grounds to believe in God? What can we know of God without recourse to revelation? What are credal statements saying? How are people constructed? How do they differ from other things? What makes for meaning or significance? What is our place in God's scheme of things? How do we best relate to God? All these questions, and others, get discussed in the present book. They also get treated with the clarity and wit characteristic of McCabe's other writings. Philosophers and theologians are not always noted for tackling such questions without recourse to jargon and without getting bogged down in details that can befog rather than illumine. Herbert McCabe, however, had the enviable ability to make his points crisply without sacrificing depth. This skill of his is as evident as ever in this new volume.

All biblical quotations below come from the New Revised Standard Version of the Bible. For assistance in preparing this book for publication I am grateful to Adam Wood, who turned some pretty illegible typescripts into a form that I could work on for editorial purposes. For expert copyediting, I am grateful to Timothy Bartel. For assistance with proofreading, I am grateful to Michael Moreland.

Brian Davies OP

1

Is Belief Wishful Thinking?

Some people think that religious belief is wishful thinking. They mean that we persuade ourselves that religious doctrines are true because we find it comforting to believe them. We would like it to be the case that the good are ultimately rewarded and the wicked punished, and so we persuade ourselves that this will really happen. We would like it to be the case that there is a wise God in charge of the world, and we cannot stand the psychological strain of doubting this, so we take up religious faith. Perhaps this does occur sometimes. Whether or not it does, I am quite sure that religious disbelief is often wishful thinking in this sense: I think that many people cease to believe because they find it too uncomfortable to think that certain doctrines are true. And, of course, whether you find the doctrine that the good and the wicked finally receive their deserts a comforting one or an uncomfortable one depends on your estimate of yourself.

But this discussion does not seem to me to be a very important one. The fact that some people get married for money is not a very important fact about marriage; it only becomes interesting if someone maintains that nobody ever gets married for love – that everybody really marries for money even when they don't admit it or even realize it. Similarly, the fact that for some people religious belief or unbelief is a matter of wishful thinking does not become interesting until someone maintains that religious belief always has to be a matter of wishful thinking – that it cannot be anything else. This stronger proposition

Statement or
affirmation about
reality

1

is, I think, interesting and false. The weaker one is perhaps true but tedious.

The proposition, then, that someone who has a religious belief holds it simply because he or she wants to seems to me to be false. But, on the other hand, there is, I think, a sense in which religious belief, like all belief, *is* wishful thinking. What I want to try to do here is to disentangle two senses of 'wishful thinking': a bad sense, in which I think religious belief isn't necessarily wishful thinking, and a good, or at least harmless sense, in which I think it is.

Perhaps I had better begin by explaining that I think that religious belief is at least a matter of accepting certain propositions as true and their contraries as false. It is true that religious beliefs are rarely simple factual beliefs of the kind that scientists might deal with, but this does not seem to me to mean that they are not true or false. They are mostly matters of fact plus interpretation, and so in any case the greater number of Christian beliefs do entail certain simple factual historical beliefs, and in their case it is certainly possible to show what scientific evidence would count against them.

Thus, for example, faith in the resurrection of Christ is a very deep and complex thing, and a great deal of theology consists simply in exploring its depths. It is not possible to comprise it in a neatly tailored formula. But whatever else it implies, it certainly entails that Christ's body did not remain in the tomb, nor was it stolen by the Apostles or anyone else, but Christ came back to life and left the tomb of his own accord. If it were shown scientifically somehow, for example, that Christ's body did in fact rot away in the tomb, then it would be shown that a proposition implied by the doctrine of the resurrection is false and therefore it would be shown that the doctrine of the resurrection is false. And, of course, part of belief in the resurrection is belief that no such scientific discovery could be made – just as it is part of the belief that the earth is round that it cannot be scientifically proved to be flat. There are, of course, other Christian beliefs which do not entail scientific facts about the world, but these also, I think, are true as opposed to being false.

It is necessary to say these things because some philosophers have held that we cannot properly use 'true' and 'false' of any propositions except those of a class known as 'empirical propositions' – roughly, the kind which can be tested by a scientific experiment or (perhaps) by observation. Some of these philosophers (who were called 'logical positivists') maintained that if it is impossible to point to the scientific evidence logical positivism upon which a proposition is based, then unless it is a useful tautology (like the propositions of logic or mathematics), it is meaningless and worthless, or as they put it, 'metaphysical'. The difficulty with this view is, of course, that it is impossible to point to the scientific evidence upon which is based the logical positivist's own proposition that only empirical propositions can be true or false. Thus, by their own account their own philosophical propositions are meaningless and worthless, and even, alas, metaphysical.

Most of the people who held logical positivist views were quite happy to see the traditional religious doctrines going down the drain as meaningless and metaphysical, but there were some of this cast of mind who still wanted to retain the use of the traditional religious sayings. They formed the theory that since these did not express empirical propositions, they were acceptable not because they were true but for some other reason. They carried the public school taboo on discussing religion to its extreme limit. To argue about religion was not only bad form but bad philosophy. They protected their religious doctrines from sceptical attack at the cost of emptying them of any assertive character at all.

There are no logical positivists left these days, and philosophers no longer place these narrow limits on the proper use of 'true' and 'false'. But it is still slightly suspect in some religious circles to claim that the articles of faith are just simply true.

This, however, is the position I want to maintain. If then you think, as I do, that to believe a doctrine, to have faith in it, means at least to hold that a certain proposition is true and not false (it means a lot more than this, but it means *at least* this), then you have a certain question to answer: how is this way of holding a proposition to be true different from and related to other ways of holding a proposition to be true? How is faith in a proposition different from or related to having reasons for holding a proposition?

Here people might take up one of two opposite positions, both of which I think are wrong. They might say (a) that having faith in a proposition has nothing whatever to do with having reasons for it, or else they might say (b) that it is exactly the same as having reasons for it.

Let's look at (a) first: to hold a proposition by faith is entirely unlike holding it for good reasons. I think that if people said this we should be inclined to wonder what they meant by saying that they held a proposition by faith as *true*. How, after all, do they *know* that they hold it as true? What is the difference between using a sentence as an assertion and using it to express an emotion? We are sometimes inclined to suppose that the difference is immediately evident to us when we use the sentence. In the one case we use it and have an assertive feeling inside us, and in the other case we use it with an expressive feeling inside us. But this is certainly not the case. Imagine people who say, 'The only thing to do with hooligan teenagers is to flog them.' These people may genuinely feel that they are making an assertion which they believe to be true. Yet what happens if their friends succeed in introducing into their minds the suspicion that they may be simply voicing their indignation at the behaviour of certain youngsters? It begins to worry them. They ask, 'Do we really think this is true, or are we merely expressing a feeling?' How do they answer this question? Certainly not by introspecting their feelings. They ask themselves, 'Have we paid much attention to the studies of ways of preventing crime?', 'Have we asked ourselves what we should flog people for?', and so on.

If people were totally indifferent to any possible reasons for asserting or denying their proposition, we should think that they didn't really hold it as true, but perhaps just liked the sound of the words used in expressing it. Thus someone might seem to assert the proposition that there was a young man of Calcutta who coated his tonsils with butter, thus converting his snore from a horrible roar to a soft oleaginous mutter. But, as soon as it became evident that the person saying this did not care at all about the evidence for or against this being the case, we should realize that he or she merely liked saying that kind of thing (enjoyed reciting limericks). In the same way, if somebody holds a doctrine on faith and is totally indifferent to any evidence for or against it, we should think that he or she did not hold it on faith as true.

At the other extreme, if someone is so concerned with reasons for and against holding his or her proposition that the holding of it is *entirely* dependent on the *reasons*, we should begin to wonder why he or she claimed to have faith in it. Faith in a proposition must surely mean more than simply estimating that there is good reason to think that it is true.

It seems to me that there is a middle way between holding, on the one hand, that faith has absolutely *nothing* to do with reasons and argument, and, on the other hand, that it is nothing *but* a matter of reasons and argument. The first extreme makes the notion of truth inapplicable. The other makes the notion of faith inapplicable.

I have already suggested that there is at least this much connection between faith in a proposition and reasoning about it: that part of belief in a proposition is belief that there is no genuine knockdown argument to *disprove* it. If I believe that Christ is God, then I must believe that he cannot be proved not to be God. At the very least, believers must hold that their beliefs cannot be shown to be logically inconsistent: thus for example to believe *both* that God is omnipotent and that human beings are free and responsible is, among other things, to believe that these two propositions cannot be shown to be inconsistent with each other. For if they are inconsistent, then at least one of them is false, and my holding them by faith couldn't be called holding them *as true*. It is therefore perfectly fair for an atheist determinist who accepts neither of these propositions nevertheless to attack the Christian on the ground that if one is true the other cannot be. It is necessary to say this, because there are some Christians who say that beliefs can, and indeed must be, absurd in the sense of repugnant to reason, logically inconsistent. For these theologians the whole point of genuine faith is that it supersedes mere human reason and defeats it. I do not think that these people take sufficiently seriously the point that faith means holding something as *true* – they think of faith as more an act of courage or trust in a very general sense.

It is not merely by showing logical inconsistencies, however, that an opponent may attack believers in their beliefs, for of course, one may try to show simply that the beliefs are contrary to fact. To believe a proposition, then, is to believe that both these kinds of attacks will fail. Of course, this belief that the attacks will fail is a belief about the proposition, not about the believer. Believers do not predict that they or anyone else will always be able to see through the arguments brought against their belief. They merely believe that the arguments in question shall be, in principle, soluble. Suppose that I believe that I am in Paris. Part of this belief is that there is no genuine proof that I am not – though I think that if someone bought me enough beer I could fairly easily be convinced that I was in London or Istanbul. Believers do not even predict that they will personally be unconvinced by specious arguments against their beliefs; they merely believe that they would be in error if they were so convinced.

All this that I have said could be the case if that actual content of our faith, the propositions which we believe, concerned the behaviour of subatomic particles in some remote galaxy about which we had no information at all except a revelation from God. But in fact, of course, faith is not the least bit like this. The theologian says that faith is a sharing in God's self-knowledge and we begin to know God by looking at his plan for human history through God's eyes. Faith is essentially a matter of recognizing certain historical events as part of God's plan of redemption, and of interpreting them correctly in terms of our salvation. We would not know how to interpret them if God had not told us. God reveals himself in history and also tells us how to interpret this history. This divine interpretation of divine history is the Bible. Now this means that the content of faith is a human content, a matter of human history, and not a matter of remote uncheckable events at the back of the moon. For this reason I think there is a closer connection still between faith and argument. So far I have spoken of believers resisting and dissolving the arguments brought against their position, but I also think that there may be arguments for their position, though not, of course, knockdown arguments. There may be what Newman called 'converging probabilities' arguments which, while not absolutely convincing, not making the truth manifestly and certainly clear, yet point towards it.

Thus someone might argue on grounds of historical evidence that there is certainly something of a puzzle about what happened after Christ died and was buried, and that the evidence does seem to point to the truth of the Apostles' story that he rose from the dead – that, at any rate, it certainly points away from any other solution that has been thought up. Of course, this doesn't prove that the resurrection happened.

In the first place, historical evidence is never absolute, knockdown, compelling evidence that anything happened. One interpretation of the evidence is usually more plausible than most of the others, sometimes it is overwhelmingly likely, but there is always the possibility, however faint, that one of the others may be more correct.

In the second place, for an event like the resurrection we should need far better evidence than we need for an event like the Norman invasion of England. This is because, taken in isolation, the resurrection of a dead man is so wildly improbable. When the corpse disappears in a detective story, the last thing we think of is that it has come back to life. We do not regard this as a possible solution on a par with others. 'Did the murderer hide it?' 'Was the man who said he saw it lying or mistaken?' 'Was the apparent corpse really dead?' We would accept all these as reasonable possibilities worth investigating. It would not even occur to us to investigate the chances of a resurrection. So only the most cast-iron evidence would serve to convince us of it in isolation.

If Charlie says that it is snowing, this is only good evidence for the fact that it is snowing if it is more likely for it to be snowing than for Charlie to be lying. The more unlikely it is to be snowing (suppose it is high summer, for example) the more sure you have to be of Charlie's reliability before you can accept his evidence. When you get something as improbable as resurrection from the dead, you need a great deal of weighty evidence before it could be said to be proved, even in the mild sense in which we speak of proving things historically. Of course I am here speaking of the resurrection in isolation, as a separate disconnected event. In actual fact the resurrection occurred in a definite context: it was only one event, although the climax, in a series of events, in a whole story. When you see the whole story you see that the resurrection, so far from being improbable, was just what was to be expected.

Think of the story of the two disciples on the road to Emmaus. They were sorrowful because Christ had been killed, but Christ met them though they did not recognize him, and he said to them: 'Oh, how foolish you are, and how slow of heart to believe all that the prophets have declared! Was it not necessary that the Messiah should suffer these things and then enter into his glory?' (Lk. 24.25–6). After the event, believers can see that they ought to have expected it; they see it in its context as forming part of the pattern of God's plan. Indeed, if they do not see it as part of this plan, as having a context in which it plays a part, there is almost no content to their belief. If it were possible merely to convince a man of the resurrection of Christ as an isolated fact, without its context, he would simply regard it as one of the extraordinary things that sometimes happen. It would not have any religious significance.

What then is the value of arguments for the articles of faith? It is difficult to give a general answer to a question like this, but I should say that they do at least show that the believer is not crazy or eccentric or unreasonable in holding his view. They show that he is not like someone who holds that the whole of Homer was written in the sixteenth century by fiendishly clever scholars who forged innumerable manuscripts. They show that he is not like Philip Henry Gosse (1810–88), who believed that the world was only 6,000 years old and that the fossils which appeared to be much older had been put there by God 6,000 years ago. Such unusual individuals have a technique for disqualifying contrary evidence. They know beforehand how they will be able to nullify any possible evidence. The man who believes that all demands for income tax really come from some immensely cunning and powerful personal enemies of his knows beforehand that anyone who tries to persuade him that this is not so is really a dupe or a member of the conspiracy. Christians have no such technique for dealing with the objections, though they do believe that all objections can be answered somehow. They are not insulated from contact with evidence in the way that the lunatic is.

I have spoken a good deal about reasons and arguments because it is here precisely that wishful thinking in the bad sense comes in. It is when people want something to be true and persuade themselves that it is true to such an extent that they accept phoney arguments for it and reject good arguments against it that we say they are indulging in wishful thinking in the bad sense. They are allowing their desires to trespass in a field that belongs exclusively to reason. If I find it comforting or exciting to think that the resurrection happened, and if I allow this emotion to influence me in such a way that I think that bad arguments for it are good ones, or so that I overlook or play down awkward evidence, then I am indeed indulging in wishful thinking. And this you sometimes find in Christian apologetics – though I think it is much commoner among people who find it detestable that the resurrection should have happened and thus distort their thinking the other way. But that is merely a matter of statistics.

Yet suppose that people do not think any of this. Suppose that they assess the worth of every argument and piece of evidence as calmly and objectively as they can, without allowing any wishful thinking to distort their judgement. Given the most favourable circumstances, such people could at the most come to the conclusion that a good deal of the Christian story is a very likely tale. They might entertain it as a plausible hypothesis. And this is all that they would be justified in doing on the evidence they have.

But Christians, of course, do not do anything of the kind. They do not say, 'These things are highly probable.' They say that they are quite certain about them. This certainty about them Christians call faith. This certainty cannot be justified by the evidence.

An important thing to notice here is that faith is not only a way of accepting the Christian story. It is also itself an important element in the story. A great deal of what we accept in faith is about faith itself. We believe that it is essential to believe. The demand which God places upon us is not that we should be well informed about his plan, but that we should believe in him. That is why I was careful to say that a detached enquirer might come to the conclusion that a *good deal* of the Christian story is a very plausible hypothesis. People who held it as a plausible hypothesis that Christ rose from the dead, and who also held it as a plausible hypothesis that this ought *not* to be held merely as a plausible hypothesis, would be in a curiously complicated (though perhaps not impossible) logical position.

Suppose we admitted that the Christian is not a wishful thinker in the sense of reasoning dishonestly. Isn't there something very like wishful thinking in having certainty when it cannot be warranted by the evidence? Christians, for example, are quite certain that no evidence will come up to disprove the resurrection. Isn't this just because they would hate to see any such evidence and therefore refuse to contemplate the possibility of there being any? Well, no. I do not think it is wishful thinking in that sense. What makes Christians so sure that no evidence will come up to prove that the resurrection didn't happen is just their conviction that the resurrection *did* happen. My being sure that I am, say, in Paris logically entails being sure that at no time, not even in the remotest future, will evidence appear to prove that I was not in Paris. No special power of prophecy is needed for this. It is just a logical requirement – just as I do not need to be a prophet to know that in any week you care to choose, Thursday will come before Friday.

All the same, I think the believer's certainty is wishful thinking in another sense. It is important to remember here that as far as the evidence goes people may be in doubt about the truth of Christian doctrines. Now what makes them certain? I think we can best understand this by looking at some cases of uncertainty.

Fred is going off for the weekend and leaving his house empty. He is just going out of the gate when he thinks, 'I wonder if I really locked the front door?' He goes back and gives it a tug. Yes, it seems locked. He starts off again. Then comes the thought, 'Did I really tug it properly?' Back he goes again. Another, harder, tug. OK. But once more a nagging suspicion. Better try the key. So he unlocks it and locks it again. Off again.

Then: 'Did I really unlock it and lock it again, or did I just lock it and then *unlock* it again?' And so on, and so on.

If we find Fred in this predicament, we do not recommend him to get some more evidence. We do not try to argue with him; we try to persuade him. At least in the early stages of this sort of scrupulosity we say, 'Pull yourself together', or 'For heaven's sake, don't be silly', or, if we are in a position of authority, we might simply forbid him to go on looking for evidence again. We think that his state of uncertainty is a pathological neurotic one, and we try to help him to feel certain, to make the necessary effort of will.

It is in this way that an element of will, hence of *wish*, enters into our certainties about matters about which we do not have enough evidence to be absolutely sure. To a very great extent we *decide* to think this rather than that. Normally no *effort* of will is required, so we only notice the wishfulness of our thinking when we find someone who lacks the element of decision, who is neurotically unable to make up his or her mind. We don't ordinarily need an effort of will to do things that are wishful. To love someone, for example, is clearly a matter of willing, but no effort is normally needed. Indeed, when we say we are willing to do so and so, we precisely mean that we will *not* need to force ourselves to it.

It seems to me that most of our opinions are wishful thinking in just this sense, not in the sense that we force ourselves to think such and such, but in the sense that we *decide* to think such and such. And life would be impossible without these wishful thinkings. It is because the uncertain man tends to disrupt social life that we think he is in a bad condition. Sometimes we think his bad condition is his own fault – in which case we blame him. Sometimes we do not, in which case we merely try to cure him. But we recognize that in either case he ought not to be in this state. The most obvious example of this is the jealousy and mutual suspicion that can destroy a family, a society or a particular personal relationship. We think of this as a bad thing and (normally) as a blameworthy thing. A man *ought* not to be constantly demanding proofs and employing private detectives.

I instance these cases of human trust and human faith not as the same thing as divine faith, but simply to show how the will and responsibility (moral responsibility) enters into belief. It is a romantic myth that there is some kind of moral superiority about people who refuse to make up their minds because the evidence is not 100 per cent compelling. We have seen too many people who have insisted that we can't be absolutely *sure* that the Jews were persecuted in Germany, that apartheid was hideously unjust, that Catholics are persecuted in some places, that prisoners are tortured in others, and so on. We do not admire such people as detached and critical intellectuals. We think that they are silly and morally at fault. Of course, it would be absurd, and a kind of idolatry, to suggest that a man ought to have the kind of certainty about his wife's honesty, or about various press reports, that he has about the creed. I am not comparing the certainty of the two cases, but merely their wishfulness.

If it is claimed that the will or wishfulness enters into belief, it is a fair question to ask, 'What is willed? What is wanted?' If we blame people for not having a certain belief on the grounds of failure of their will, what is it that they have not wanted enough?

Let us look at the jealous husband. The good esteem that others have of us is one of our possessions. We do a good deal of work to acquire it, and we are harmed if it is damaged. It exists, of course, in other people's minds, and may or may not be expressed in their behaviour. To think ill of somebody is already to harm them, even if the thought is not made public. This must be so because there would be no harm in *speaking* ill of people unless it made others *think* ill of them. The jealous husband damages his wife's esteem in his own mind. He is likely to do more than this as a consequence, but first of all he harms her by thought itself. Now to love someone means to desire

13

good for them and not harm, hence suspicion and mistrust are opposed to love. So we blame the jealous man because he does not sufficiently want the good of his wife. The trouble with the unbeliever is the much more serious one that he does not sufficiently want the good of himself.

The good of one's wife is a relative and finite thing. It can be compared with other goods, and it may have to be sacrificed for some other good. A man may have to decide between allowing his wife to be shot and revealing secrets to the Gestapo. A man may find evidence so compelling that as a matter of intellectual honesty he has to give up the good esteem of his wife. Of course, many of the things that are good for a man himself are also relative goods which may have to be sacrificed; a man's comfort and peace of mind and for that matter his continued life are all things he normally wants, but things that he may sensibly be prepared to give up for the sake of greater goods. But his own ultimate good, his own final happiness, is absolute; it is that for the sake of which other, relative goods can be sacrificed. People can refuse any good you care to mention. There is no finite good that they are absolutely determined to want, unless they are sick. Indeed, we regard it as a sign of mental illness when people seem to be unable to refuse some particular good.

Now the central thing that a Christian believes is that God has intervened in his creation in such a way that we have a personal relationship with him. God has not merely created us, but has also spoken with us and revealed himself to us. It is the things that God has said about God that are the objects of faith. The way in which God has chosen to communicate his self-knowledge is by entering history and by giving to us in the scriptures an authentic interpretation of this.

Now since Christians believe that revelation is a matter of a personal relationship with God, they also believe that lack of faith is comparable with the neurotic suspicions of a jealous man. They say that as a result of what God has in fact done to the world, as a result of the incarnation, faith in God is normal in the sense that marital trust is normal. It is lack of faith that is the abnormal.

But, of course, all this is a matter of what the Christian believes. Given that the world is as the Christian says it is, then faith is justifiable wishful thinking. The will enters into the thinking not to disrupt the intelligence but to unite persons. ⌈Given that the world is the way the Christian says it is, the non-believer is like the man who refuses to accept the fact that his door is locked, or the jealous husband always neurotically searching for an illusory final argument.⌋ He ought to believe and does not. But, of course, all this is not something that the non-believer can accept without becoming a believer. Non-believers can come to see that they ought to believe, but only by becoming believers. One could not first convince someone that they have a duty to believe, and then stand back and say 'OK, go on, do it.' One cannot believe that one has a duty to believe except by believing already.

The positions of believers and non-believers are both, in this sense, self-justifying. If you think the creed is true, then you think it ought to be believed. If on the other hand you do not think it is true, you do not think it ought to be believed. Notice here the difference between the creed and, say, a scientific truth. If you think that water boils at 100 degrees at normal pressure, it does not follow that you think it ought to be believed (you may not care). You may think people are the happier for not knowing this sinister truth. At most, you think people who do not believe it are *mistaken*, not *guilty*. But just because faith is a matter of the good sort of wishful thinking, a matter of a personal relationship with God, it does follow from the fact that it is true that we *ought* to believe it. An interesting corollary is that though the believer thinks that the creed (because it is true) ought to be believed, the unbeliever does not necessarily think that (because of its falsehood) it ought to be *disbelieved*. In fact, unbelievers *do* usually think this. They usually do regard the creed as a dangerous and sinister and harmful piece of falsehood. But they may not. They might restrict themselves to the negative proposition that it is not the case that we *ought* to believe it. They may even think that as a matter of fact it is good for some people to believe it, even though it is not true.

If I may sum up the position I have been trying to maintain:

1. Faith means thinking that some propositions are true, as opposed to being false.
2. To hold a proposition to be true by faith is neither simply to hold that there are good reasons for accepting it, nor, on the other hand, is it something that has nothing whatever to do with reasons for holding the proposition.
3. Wishful thinking in the bad sense means allowing your desires to influence you so that you think a bad argument is a good one. Wishful thinking in this sense has to do with *arguments*. If faith were a matter of accepting propositions on the basis of argument, it would simply be bad for it to be a matter of wishful thinking.
4. But faith involves being more certain about the truth of a proposition than is warranted by any arguments for it.
5. Given that the Christian's picture of the world is true, then this certainty is comparable to the certainty a man normally has of his wife's affections, i.e. it is a certainty for which we do not demand or approve of evidence. Lack of certainty in faith is like unreasonable jealousy.
6. This similarity is due to the fact that both are a matter of personal relationship, and therefore involve will and decision – not necessarily an effort of will.
7. Of course, all this is only plausible if Christians are right, if their picture of the world *is* true. It will not hold if their picture is untrue.
8. Non-believers may come to think that Christian beliefs are reasonable or plausible and remain unbelievers. They cannot come to think that they ought to believe, without ceasing to be unbelievers.

2

Are Creeds Credible?

There is no doubt that faith is a bit of a nuisance. Wouldn't life be a lot simpler without it? Why can't we just accept what seems reasonable to us, reject what seems unreasonable, and be mildly sceptical about the rest? This surely would be the civilized attitude, the attitude of the independent mind, a mind which is neither credulous nor arrogant, but coolly prepared to face the truth when it appears, and to confront its own ignorance when that appears. But the faith business seems alien to all this.

We can't help feeling that what has happened is something like this. Once upon a time, before we had perfected our modern critical techniques, when it was a lot easier to make mistakes about the world and human beings, there were a certain number of beliefs which it was quite reasonable to hold, and these were taught by men of authority and status. Gradually, however, there developed new ways of looking at the world and it began to be seen that the old views were inaccurate and out of date. But by this time there was a large vested interest in these views – there was a whole priestly class, for example, whose status and even livelihood depended on the acceptance of the old views. These people were only human, and naturally they felt it was a bad thing that the traditional opinions were being questioned, so they spread about the idea that it was a bad thing to question. Since it was no longer really possible to show that these old opinions were reasonable, the priestly class invented the idea of faith; we were to stick to the ancient beliefs but were now to hold them out of loyalty to a tradition, by faith instead of reasons. Of course this wasn't a deliberate plot to fool people. It was a more or less unconscious reaction on the part of a social class which needed to safeguard its position. You might ask how other people came to be taken in by this move. Well, part of the reason is that the modern world is rather frightening – not just our modern world but the modern world in any age. To keep up with the age we have to stretch ourselves to the utmost; we have to be adult and independent, and this is rather difficult. It is sometimes a lot easier to contract out, to live on nostalgia for the past. The religious beliefs which we are asked to take on faith come from an older time which seems to us more peaceful, less nerve-shattering than our own. These beliefs postulate a cosy intelligible world, rather like the world of the nursery when life was so much simpler, so a lot of people welcome the idea of faith because they are afraid to think for themselves, and all of us at one time or another have a hankering after this return to childhood.

This is, I think, a reasonably fair statement of a belief about beliefs which is pretty common these days. It was perhaps commoner in the last century than in this, but it is still widespread. It goes usually, in England at any rate, with a pleasant tolerance of religion. Some people hold that religion in fact is a good thing, this occasional indulgence in childishness is refreshing, it is good for mental health to relax in this way; no doubt this is why so many excellent philosophers and scientists and other highly intelligent people still maintain religious beliefs.

This is a belief which, as I say, goes with a great tolerance of religion and also an unfathomable ignorance of what exactly religious beliefs are, and of how religious people think. I do not myself find it to be a very plausible account of the history of religious ideas. I think that one of the reasons why people cling to it in spite of its implausibility is that they find the idea of faith not only a nuisance but irrelevant. It is not so much the content of the creeds that bothers them as the fact that they are *creeds*. They feel they must give themselves some account of the idea of *faith* itself, to make it fit somehow into the human picture; and their explanation briefly is that the contents of the creed are so out of date and unlikely that they can only be held by faith: that was how faith was invented.

Because so many people honestly think this, I should like here to offer an alternative account of the relevance of faith. Why do we have faith at all? What is the theologian's account of faith? Let us come at it not first of all from the point of view of people who have not got it and for whom it is something strange and alien. Let us begin from the point of view of those who do have faith. What account do they give? Here we have to go back a long way. In fact we have literally to go back to the beginning.

God made creatures of all kinds, with all kinds of powers and capabilities. Human beings do certain things. They eat, laugh, get angry and do crossword puzzles; they explore the Antarctic or make Sputniks or string quartets, and we are delighted but not surprised. We say, 'Naturally, that is the kind of thing that people do.' Similarly tigers eat and get angry, and again we are not surprised. We say it is natural enough, it is just what we should expect of a tiger. Different kinds of behaviour are natural to different kinds of things. When a horse behaves like a horse we think it quite natural, but if a man behaves like a horse we are surprised and ask for an explanation. So if X behaves like a horse, and we think it natural for X to behave like a horse, then this is because we think X is a horse. If we don't think it natural for X to be horsing around, it is because X is not a horse. A horse is just a thing which *by nature* behaves like a horse.

Can we give an account of what is natural to human beings? This is notoriously difficult. Remember that we mean 'what is natural to humans as humans'. Some people think of 'natural' behaviour as simply the kind of behaviour that we have in common with other animals, but here we mean any behaviour at which we have no need to be surprised. In this sense it is just as natural for people to build a nuclear power station as it is for them to eat and sleep. We are not astonished at any of these things in the way that we would be completely astonished if, for example, a horse were to write a sonnet. We are lost in admiration for scientists, but we do not think they have superhuman powers; if a horse wrote a poem we would certainly think it had super-equine powers.

As people get better and better at controlling their environment it becomes increasingly difficult to set limits and say, 'Well, anyway it could never be natural for a human being to do *that*', as we can fairly easily predict that it will never be natural for a tiger to do *that*. Five hundred years ago, if you suggested that someone might launch his or her own private moon, people might have believed you, but they would have said, 'Yes, someone might do that by magic, or by being in league with the devil, or by a miracle.' What they wouldn't have believed is that someone could do such a thing quite naturally, in perfectly natural ways. Yet this we now know is the case. But whatever we may be able to do now or in the future, whatever may come naturally to us, there is one thing which could never be natural to us. We could not be naturally divine.

Remember, I pointed out that if something behaves like a horse naturally, then it is a horse; and similarly if man behaved like God by nature, it would be because he is God. If it were ever 'perfectly natural' for a man to have a divine nature as it is perfectly natural for him to elaborate quantum mechanics, then he would be God. God is the only being which is by nature divine. Not even the omnipotent God could make a creature which was by nature divine. It is not that God cannot make lesser creatures easily enough, but he finds greater creatures a bit more difficult, and finally finds it impossible to make a creature with the same nature as himself. It is not a question of difficulty. When we say that God could make a creature with the same nature as himself, we are saying the same sort of thing as when we say he couldn't make a square circle. God couldn't make a square circle, not because he is not powerful enough, but because a square circle is a contradiction, something that couldn't be made; the phrase 'square circle' is a self-cancelling one, it could not be the name of anything. In the same way, a creature which is by nature divine is a contradiction; it is a creature which is uncreated, and the phrase 'uncreated creature' could not be the name of anything.

But the astonishing teaching of Christianity is that God has, so to speak, done the next best thing. He could not make man by nature divine, but he has given him divinity as a gift. This is what we call grace. We do share in the divine nature, we do behave like God, but not by nature. We can do what God does, but in God it is natural, in us it is not – we call it supernatural. Just as it would be supernatural to a horse to write a poem, so it is supernatural to a human being to behave like God. This means that our divinity must always come as a surprise, some-thing eternally astonishing. We could never get used to it and say: 'Well, naturally enough'.

Now one of the things that sharing in God's life involves is sharing in his knowledge of himself. This share in God's self-knowledge is called faith, it is a kind of knowledge we have not by nature (we never could have it by nature) but as a gift. It is because faith is part of our divinity, and because our divin-ity can never be *natural* to us (it can only be natural to God), that faith cannot be quite assimilated into ordinary reasonable human life.

What does it mean to share in somebody else's knowledge? Especially somebody else's self-knowledge? Before answering this, I must further explain that faith is only the beginning of our share in God's self-knowledge. It is a very imperfect kind of sharing. Our sharing will not be complete and perfect until we see God in heaven. As a way of knowing, faith is the lowest kind of knowledge, much inferior to human science; it is only superior to science, and more important, because of the things that we know by faith, and the fact that finally it will develop into the vision of God.

Again, what does it mean to share in somebody else's knowledge? Well, we can best understand this by comparison with the ordinary way in which one of us can share in another's knowledge – the business of teaching. Take a boy at school. He learns from his teacher. He comes to believe certain things because his teacher has told him. He is beginning to share in the teacher's knowledge, but for the moment he only shares in it in a very imperfect way. For the moment he simply believes it on authority – because the teacher has said so. He has not thought it out for himself. He merely has faith. When he grows up he sheds this faith and begins to have opinions which are really his own. This, I take it, is the essential difference between adult education and a school. A school is a place for training. A university is a place for discussion. In a school we try to get a child to believe the fundamental things that society recognizes as true and important. In a university we try to carry on a continuous critical discussion. (That incidentally is the reason why there are good arguments for having Catholic schools in a non-Catholic state, but none whatsoever for having a Catholic university.)

The point is that coming to share the knowledge of another means beginning with faith in the other person. There has to be a basis of faith on which to build. There are, as you know, children who are handicapped and unable to learn and grow up, simply because they lack this fundamental sense of security and trust in the adult world, the faith in the teacher which is a prime necessity. But of course, the purpose of this faith is to bring the child to maturity when it will cease to have faith, when it will lose its dependence on the teacher and be able to think things out for itself.

Notice that to shed your faith in your teachers does not necessarily mean to disagree with them – though, in fact, normal

people go through a period of reaction against the actual beliefs they have been brought up in; it is the simplest way of
manifesting the changeover from belief to independent knowledge. But such coming to maturity does not necessarily mean
disagreeing with the teacher. You may go on holding the same
opinions, but now hold them as a matter of your own judgement and no longer as a matter of faith.

These two stages, first faith and then seeing things for yourself, take place also in the matter of sharing in God's knowledge.
But here it is not a matter of growing up in our human life, but
of growing up in our divine life. The point of maturity, when
we lose our faith and see for ourselves, is the point at which
we begin to see God in heaven.

Now somebody might want to object that this confirms all
their worst suspicions. They always thought that religion was a
matter of childishness, of a sort of arrested development which
keeps us in the schoolroom throughout our lives, unable to
think for ourselves. And here we are admitting it.

In answer to this I should say that there is such a thing as
arrested development in human things (and a very bad thing it
is) when people refuse to think for themselves and look around
for some human authority to tell them what to think. Such
people are afraid of the responsibilities of growing up. They
want to remain children for ever – like the loathsome Peter
Pan. What is wrong with such people is that when they have
an opportunity of thinking for themselves they refuse it and
cling to their faith. They are offered a higher and more mature
way of knowing, but they won't have it.

In divine things, however, this is not the situation. These are
things that we *cannot know any other way* expect by having
faith in the teacher, God, who tells us about them. They are not
things we could find out for ourselves. They are not the kind
of things we could naturally know. Our knowledge of them is
super-natural. We are not refusing an offered opportunity, we
are not avoiding a higher, more grown-up approach, because

there is in this life no higher way available. The boy who refuses to have faith in the teacher *may* be acquiring a grown-up critical sense and beginning to think for himself, or he *may* be simply refusing to learn. I imagine it must be one of a teacher's most difficult jobs to decide which of these is happening. But, in the case of divine things, those who refuse to have faith are always in the latter class. They are not starting to think independently because about these things it is impossible to think independently. They are merely not thinking at all. They are not displaying their maturity. They are merely playing truant. Of course genuine arrested development, the refusal to grow up, to be mature, is possible in the divine life as in human life. People may deliberately refuse the maturity which is offered to them in the vision of God. They then remain in that state of perpetual arrested development that we call hell.

The divine life does indeed grow in us even on earth, but we never reach full maturity; we never dispense with faith until we actually see God face to face. Now the question is: what is the relation between this divine life (and divine knowledge that we call faith) and human life (and human knowledge)? Some people have held that they are actually opposed to each other. You know that kind of person who thinks that you can't be a saint unless you're very slightly ill; this sort of person tends also to think that you can't have faith unless what you believe is humanly incredible. They think of faith not as a matter of knowing or of learning, but rather as a matter of courage, a leap into the unknown, a quixotic championing of the absurd. Now faith is certainly a leap into the unknown in the sense that what you believe is something that cannot be known by ordinary human power. But it is a leap which precisely tries to make this *known*. It is not a rejection of knowledge, it is an effort to know more – to get to know more by trusting in a teacher.

There are two sets of people who think of faith as the acceptance of the absurd. People in the first set go on to say what a splendid thing faith is: it means a reaching out beyond all human criticism; the man of faith does not care about the carping objections of mere logicians, etc. People who belong to the second set go on to say what a dangerous and foolish thing faith is, and for the same reason. It seems to me, however, that both these sets of people are wrong. I would claim that our divinity (one manifestation of which is our faith) transcends our humanity, but is certainly not opposed to it. The Spirit of Christ by which we live is not destructive but creative. It does not reject anything human.

What does it mean to say that the divine life transcends the human? Simply this: that because we are divine we have a destiny, a purpose which is beyond any purpose we could have as merely human. However we envisage human fulfilment, human perfection or human happiness, our divine purpose is far beyond this, and because we have this greater end in view we organize our human life with a view to something greater than it.

Let me return to my comparison with the child and its parents or teacher. Left to themselves, children will organize their world in certain terms – this or that is important, this or that is unimportant, and so on. On the whole, the world of children will be organized in terms of their desires and pleasures and pains, though there will, of course, be hints of a larger world, a dim recognition that there is a lot more in life than all that. Now when the parent or teacher comes on the scene this enclosed world is broken into to some extent. Because of what they learn from their teachers, children will reorganize their world to some extent. They will believe that certain apparently unimportant things are really very important – like washing and learning to write. They cannot see why these are immensely important, but normally, and if they have the right sort of relationship with their teachers, they will believe that they are, and be prepared to sacrifice their own scale of values for their sake. Their purpose as potential adults transcends their child's purpose, but again, because they really are children and really are potential adults, there is no fundamental opposition between the two. Education does not *have* to make children miserable. There have been educationalists who thought that you were not really educating children unless they were doing something they actively disliked. These are like the people who think that faith has to be absurd. On the other hand, of course, there have been people who thought just the opposite: that you are not really educating children unless they do what they like. These are like the people who say that there can be no belief which transcends any human reason. This is a refusal to believe that the adult world transcends the child world.

The divine life, therefore, because it transcends human life, will involve some reorganization of human life towards a larger world, the world of eternity. But here we meet an additional complication. It is not just a matter of reorienting human life because a certain amount of repair work is needed first. Briefly, according to Christian belief, man was created with divine life as well as his human life, but he lost his divinity by the Fall, and this also damaged his humanity. The result of this is that we need to make certain efforts of reorganization even to lead a properly human life, never mind a divine one. In fact without the grace of divine life we are so enfeebled that we cannot even manage the job of living a human life. We have so much tendency to wishful thinking, to taking as true what we would like to be true, that if we try to run our lives simply on the basis of what seems good to us, we are liable to act in a less than human way. Even in order to live a human life, therefore, we need to make certain sacrifices, to give up things that seem at first sight desirable, to do a certain amount of violence to what look like ordinary human tendencies.

It is merely by extension of this that our divine super-natural life demands certain sacrifices, but what it does not and cannot demand is a sacrifice of the fundamentally human things. It cannot make demands which are really contrary to human dignity, for it is a *super*natural, not a *sub*natural life that is in question. It may make demands which seem at first sight to be contrary to human dignity, but this will be merely because we do not know all the facts. Thus a man may suffer all kinds of indignities rather than deny his faith, and this may seem absurd to those who do not know all the facts (i.e. do not themselves believe). But the supernatural life can never make demands which are genuinely contrary to human dignity. Above all, it cannot demand that we do what is wicked or believe what is false. The divine teacher does not tell us things which are self-contradictory or false. It is always possible to show even to someone who does not believe in any article of faith that these do not involve an absurdity. Christians must, it seems to me, believe that it is always possible to dissolve any argument brought *against* their beliefs; this itself is a matter of their faith. That creeds are not *incredible* is itself a part of the *creed*. In this minimal sense of reasonable, in which we mean 'not unreasonable', faith is certainly reasonable. Nobody can produce an absolute knockdown argument to show that the believer is talking nonsense. Of course, someone may produce an argument which seems to me knockdown. It is no part of the faith that all believers will be able to answer all possible objections against the creed. But it is part of the faith that any objection is answerable in principle.

I think that nowadays quite a lot of people would be prepared to accept this. They would grant that Christianity does somehow always manage to elude the critic (just when he thinks it caught in a nice contradiction, theology somehow slips through the logical net). They are prepared to grant that, in this sense, Christianity is not unreasonable – it is not sheer nonsense. But the Christian often goes further, and certainly I would want to go further. I would claim not only that Christianity is logically coherent but that also it is reasonable, in the sense that if people consider it coolly and calmly and objectively, there is a very good chance of them coming to believe in it. Of course most people these days don't have much of a chance of considering anything at all, even a detergent, coolly and calmly and reasonably. But there are some circumstances where this ought to be possible. I do not say that any investigator will find knockdown arguments to prove that Christianity is true; indeed I am sure that this cannot happen – just as sure as I am that there are no knockdown arguments against it, for we are dealing with the supernatural, which cannot be arrived at by merely logical means. The kind of argument one has in this sort of matter is not a simple linear argument from these premisses through these means to that conclusion. What you have, as Newman pointed out, is a convergence of arguments each pointing towards the conclusion but none of them absolutely settling it. This is the case in all human studies – history, for example. The sort of argument by which someone may come near to Christianity is much more like an historical argument than a mathematical one.

Now there are some people who will admit even this. They will admit that Christianity is reasonable even in this sense, that it is not merely logically coherent, but also a pretty reasonable hypothesis. They will admit that there is a lot of evidence of one kind and another to suggest that Christian beliefs are true, just as there is a lot of evidence of one kind and another to suggest that telepathy is quite common or that Queen Elizabeth I was in love with Essex. What they find so unreasonable in Christians is that, instead of saying that Christianity is highly probable, they claim to be completely certain. When you do establish something by this kind of probable and convergent argument, you have every right to hold it as your opinion, but you have no right to claim absolute certainty and to be sure that you will never meet a genuine refutation of it. This is what finally seems unreasonable about faith to the openminded liberal sceptic. And here I can agree with him. In this sense I am prepared to admit that you might call faith unreasonable.

It is not unreasonable in the sense that it is absurd or incoherent. Nor is it unreasonable in the sense that there are not good reasons for it. But it is, if you like, unreasonable in that it demands a *certainty* which is not warranted by the reasons. I am completely certain that I am in Oxford at the moment. I have all the evidence I need for certainty on this point. It is true that I admit the logical possibility that I may be drugged or dreaming or involved in some extraordinarily elaborate deception. But this doesn't really affect my certainty. Yet the evidence which makes it reasonable to hold, for example, that Christ rose from the dead comes nowhere near this kind of evidence. One might say that the evidence in spite of all probability does really seem to point to this fantastic conclusion, but it is certainly not the kind of evidence which makes me quite sure and certain. And yet I am more certain that Christ rose from the dead than I am that I am in Oxford. When it comes to my being there, I am prepared to accept the remote possibility that I am the victim of an enormous practical joke. But I am not prepared to envisage any possibility of deception about the resurrection. Of course I can easily envisage my argument for the resurrection being disposed of. I can envisage myself being confronted by what seems to me to be unanswerable arguments against it. But this is not the same thing. I am prepared to envisage myself ceasing to believe in it, but I am not prepared to envisage either that there really are unanswerable arguments against it or that I would be justified in ceasing to believe it. All this is because, although reasons may lead me to belief, they are not the basis of my belief. I believe certain things because God has told them to me, and I am able to believe them with certainty and complete assurance only because of the divine life within me. It is a gift of God that I believe, not something I can achieve by human means.

It is important to see that faith is not an additional reason. It is not that you can get so far with reasons and then you have to stop until faith comes along and carries you the extra bit to the end. You cannot arrive at belief *by* human reason but you can get the whole way there *with* human reason. You may come to see that it is reasonable and come to believe it with absolute certainty at one and the same moment. Or, as most of us do, you may come to believe it with certainty and afterwards find that it is quite reasonable. Or you may come to see that it is reasonable but never believe it with divine faith. A great deal of nonsense is talked about the psychology of belief on the assumption that reason and faith are always temporally distinct, that faith cannot come until one has finished with reason and waits poised on the brink to make a leap into the unknowable. This can happen, but it is only one of many possibilities and not the most common, at any rate in my experience.

Since faith means believing something because God has revealed it, the only things we can believe are things that God has revealed. Now these are of two kinds. God has first of all revealed things about himself and his plan for human salvation which we could never have known about if he had not revealed them and given us faith in his word. But God, says the Christian, has also revealed some things that we could perhaps have discovered for ourselves without his revelation. I mentioned that as a result of humanity's first rejection of divine life even our humanity itself is damaged. One of the most important results of this is the chronic disease of wishful thinking, which makes it extremely difficult to arrive at the truth even by ordinary human means, especially in anything which directly affects man himself (only consider the amount of rubbish which is talked about politics). This means that, although it is possible, it is extremely unlikely that people shall by themselves arrive at the truth in certain matters which are of the first importance for human happiness, such as the existence of God himself, and certain basic moral principles which we need to maintain our human dignity. For this reason God has revealed some of these things even though we could theoretically arrive at them by human reason. Of course, if he is to reveal anything, he must reveal his existence. You could hardly believe something because he said it if you did not also believe he existed. But, besides this, God has also revealed certain truths in ethics (e.g. the prohibition of murder) which people could have arrived at by themselves. It is important to see that if it happens that someone does arrive at these things purely by use of reason then he or she cannot be believing them. Belief means accepting truths because they have been revealed by God. If you have succeeded in proving something then you don't believe it because it is revealed; you believe for the good reasons which you have found. Thus the same proposition may be accepted by some because they have proved it, and by others because God has revealed it. What is impossible is that one and the same person at one and the same moment should both believe and know, both accept on God's word and accept for his or her own reasons. I speak here, of course, of proof. Faith is not incompatible with seeing that something is reasonable, but it is incompatible with proof. Often, of course, one cannot easily answer the question 'Do you believe this by faith or can you prove it?' I am sometimes convinced intellectually by arguments for the existence of God, and, at the moment of conviction, I suppose I do not have faith in God's existence; I have something better: knowledge. But afterwards I can say, 'Well, maybe I was being misled, perhaps there are important flaws in that argument.' But I do not for this reason doubt the existence of God. This shows that habitually I believe it rather than know it.

Finally, it is most important to see that the function of reason does not cease with the coming of faith. Faith, as I have said, is a part of our divine life. It is a share in God's self-knowledge, and it is a part of our knowledge. Although it remains something learned, although it is never something we can think out for ourselves, it is something we can think about for ourselves. This thinking about what God has told us is called theology, and this is by far the most important function of human reason in relation to faith. The apologetic function by which we seek to show up fallacies in arguments directed against our beliefs, and the preliminary function in which we try to show that it is reasonable to hold these beliefs, are both only minor jobs of the theologians. Their real business is to think about what is revealed, to see how one part fits in with another, to see the whole thing as a coherent human thing, not arbitrary slabs of information given us to 'test our faith', but all as knowledge given to us 'for us and for our salvation', as we say in the creed.

3

Doubt is Not Unbelief

I do not here wish to give some kind of psychological account
of the state of belief in general and doubt in general – if there
are such things. My focus is on Christian belief. So I think we
should begin by looking at what belief means in the sense that
we use it, say, at baptism, when the answer to the question
'What do you seek from the church?' is 'Belief'.

'I believe in God.' I don't think the best way to begin understanding this is to compare it with 'I believe there are nine
planets (though I've never counted them)' or 'I believe Australia
is there (though I've never seen it)'. I think, as I'll be saying
presently, that 'I believe in God' does have to do with believing
that some propositions are true. But I don't think you can start
there.

One way to start is with the model of a child and her parents. One thing that is necessary for the health and growth of
children is that they should believe that their parents love them.
This is almost as necessary as food and drink, and, indeed, without it the children may die because of refusing food and drink.
This belief is necessary for their health. When you hear someone say that faith is necessary for salvation, remember that this
is just the same thing in bigger words: words that reach down
to a deeper level of belief and health. [The whole of our faith is
the belief that God loves us;] I mean there isn't anything else.
Anything else we say we believe is just a way of saying that
God loves us. Any proposition, any article of faith, is only an
expression of faith if it is a way of saying that God loves us.

Have you ever thought of the extraordinary unconscious arrogance of Western Christians who think that they are being broadminded and ecumenical when they talk about the 'Great World Faiths': Hinduism, Buddhism, and so on? This is wrongly to try to squeeze these religions into a Christian mould. Buddhists don't think they have a great world faith. They are not in the least interested in faith. Nor are Hindus. Jews are, of course, and so are Muslims, but they really belong to the same family as Christians, and it is Christians who make a great fuss about faith. And this is just because they see the relation of people to God on the model of the relation of children to their parents, or to adult society in general.

Think some more about the very young child. First of all, her faith that she is loved is not something that she works out by assessing her world and coming to a conclusion. It is something *given*, taken for *granted* (in the literal sense). Indeed, if it is not granted, if she is deprived of the belief that she is loved, she will not even be *able* to assess her world at all. She will go more or less crazy.

The child doesn't arrive at or achieve her belief that she is loved. It is a precious gift which is just there, like the gift of life itself. But it can, of course, be destroyed. It is notoriously possible for adults, and especially parents, to erode a child's faith, to leave the child insecure and uncertain that she is loved, uncertain therefore of her own value, uncertain that she matters. The love of parents, and later of other friends may fail; they may betray us. Indeed, I think we have a whole society (known as the Free World) which is so structured as to destroy belief in love, to eat away at the confidence people have in each other, to replace friendship by competitiveness, generosity by domination and submission, community by national security, love by fear.

The Christian notion of God is based on a belief in a love which simply can never fail. God, for the Christian, is the lover who accepts us absolutely and unconditionally, quite regardless of whether we are nice or nasty. We put this simply by saying that God loves sinners. This is what the cross says, and that is why it is the centre of Christian faith. God cannot fail to love us, whatever we do. But we can fail to believe this.

Children, of course, quite quickly come to realize the importance of their parents' love. And, quite soon, they need to be reassured about it. It is not enough for them to be told, to be kissed and cuddled, and so on. They need to test it out. Lots of the misbehaviour of children is experimental – making sure that the love will still be there under all circumstances. I think that some of the things we class as doubt are often quite like this: testing out not so much God's love for us as our belief in it – discovering how far our faith can go. This seems to me not so much a good thing or a bad thing as an *inevitable* thing – as inevitable and necessary as the infuriating behaviour of children.

So Christianity sets great store by faith precisely because it sees our relationship to God, to the ultimate mystery behind and beyond the universe, our relationship to the Creator, the source of all being and meaning, as a personal one – not just the relationship of a work of art to the artist, of the poem to the poet, of the thing made to the maker, but of the child made to the parent. We are not just what God has made, though that is tremendous enough. We are whom God loves. This is the gospel. This is what we believe. We believe in belief, belief in God's love, as the ultimate thing about us. This is as essential to the divine life we have been called to as is a child's confidence in her parents to the human life into which she has been born.

[Faith is a kind of knowing that God loves us. It is not just a feeling or a mood, but a kind of understanding or knowing.]And knowledge, for us, is the answering of asked questions. That is why our knowledge is expressed in language and in the form of statements or propositions. People who say that faith is not 'propositional' because it is a personal relationship are, I think, very muddled. Faith is not just a feeling of happiness because of the beloved. It is what that feeling of happiness is based on.

The happiness and joy are sensible, human, awake happiness and joy (not like the happiness of being high or drunk), just because there is a reason for it. It is based on a belief, a belief that can be and has to be expressed in language – whether the language of words or of other symbols such as sacramental rites or the crucifix.

⌈Faith can be, and has to be, expressed in propositions.⌉But it isn't about these propositions; the propositions themselves have continually to be tested to make sure that they are expressions of faith and not of something else, expressions, that is, of belief in God's love for us. The trouble arises because faith, like the human persons who have it, is a communal, social thing. You cannot have faith without the community of believers and its tradition any more than you can have a human being without human society and human history. So any expression of our faith is also invariably an expression of our loyalty to, our belonging to, this tradition and community. This is not a bad thing. Indeed, it is an absolutely necessary and good thing, for faith belongs to human animals. The difficulties begin to arise (it is part of the dangerous process of eroding our faith) when we pay less attention to the doctrine as expressing our faith in the love of God for us, and concentrate simply on the doctrine as expressing our loyalty to our fellow-Christians, to the church. That is why we have to test and criticize our doctrines to question both what we are making of them and what use the church itself is making of them. Are they degenerating simply into an expression of loyalty? Are they really still about God's love?

This is a kind of doubting because it is a kind of questioning, and it is an integral part of faith itself. It is the kind of questioning that is called theology. The object of theology is to see the traditional teachings of the church as a unified whole, unified around the gospel that God loves us. Only when we see what the church teaches about sin or grace or the eucharist or the Trinity as all part of a revelation of the love of God – *only*

36

when we see this – do we begin to understand these doctrines. And the only way to see this is to question them and to question our understanding of them.

Quite often we simply cannot see the relevance of some doctrine, or we suspect that its origins lie in some power struggle in the church rather than in the preaching of the gospel. Quite often the thing seems simply unintelligible or daft. It seems to me that the sensible reaction in such cases is neither to accept the doctrine blindly simply because you were told it at school, nor to reject it uncritically for the same reason. The sensible reaction is one of questioning and doubt. It is a reaction that demands a certain amount of work and thought. It is doing theology.

Occasionally, if you do this, you will find that what you always thought was a 'teaching of the church' turns out not to be that at all but simply what a lot of past theologians have thought – the so-called doctrine of Limbo, for example. Sometimes you find that what you always took to be the meaning of the doctrine is not what it actually means: that, for example, in the eucharist the body of Christ is physically located disguised as bread – that Christ can be 'the prisoner in the tabernacle'. It is especially true of moral matters that what is called the teaching of the church often turns out to be just the prejudices of the last generation but one preserved because the church is inevitably a rather conservative and conserving institution.

Sometimes the thing will be baffling; sometimes the job of making sense of some teaching will still be quite intractable – well, you must not expect to solve all problems quickly, and here it seems to me that your acceptance of this doctrine remains dark, your faith still coexists with doubt in this area. The doctrine in question cannot be any kind of nourishment to your Christian life. It remains dormant for you. But this is not disbelief. I think a startlingly large number of Christians are this way about such absolutely central doctrines as that of the

Trinity. It is a pity, though, if you simply say: 'Well that is all very difficult, so let's just ignore it and get back to Our Lady of Fatima or the fellowship of the eucharist.' It is a pity because if you just do that the chances are that you have an inadequate and infantile view of Our Lady and of the eucharist.

None of this, though, is disbelief. Disbelief is quite other. To understand this we need to get back to our model of the child and her parents. What happens to the child who has lost faith in her parents' love? The first thing is fear – a fear that she does not matter, that she has no value or importance. This is the fear that St John says is cast out by love, by being loved, by knowing you are loved (1 Jn 4.18). The child who is deprived of love is characteristically defensive. She is terrified of admitting any inadequacy or guilt – I mean terrified of admitting it even to herself. She becomes gradually self-righteous, convinced of her rightness, with a conviction that conceals, and is meant to conceal, a deep anxiety. She is not able simply to accept herself, warts and all, as valuable because someone loves her. So she has to create a self-image for herself, a self-flattering image. She will have to protect her importance by having power over others. She will be terrified of being at the mercy of others, vulnerable to them. She will guard her self-image with possessions which make her independent of others. She will at all costs protect what she calls her 'freedom', meaning her isolation from others and the demands they might make on her. She will see the world as a place fundamentally of competition and struggle in which she has to win, rather than of friendship and cooperation.

All that is an image of disbelief. If you fail to believe that the most important and fundamental thing about you is that you are loved, if you fail to believe in God, then you have no recourse except to believe in yourself. All sin arises from the deep fear that is involved here. You only have to ask yourself why in the end you have sinned on any particular occasion. If you think hard enough and honestly enough, you will trace it back to fear: fear that you will not matter, that someone is threatening the importance or status or wealth you have carefully built up for yourself, fear that you are missing out on some experience that makes you you. Tracing sins back to their single root in such anxieties is as important as tracing all Christian doctrines back to their root in the faith that we are loved. In fact it is part of the same process. All sin is a symptom of faithlessness or uncertainty about being loved, as all belief is an affirmation of that love.

The societal and political manifestation of disbelief (of belief that we make ourselves and are only what we make ourselves) is, of course, the world of liberal individualism – the world of isolated individuals asserting their freedom against each other. And, of course, if this is what society is like, you need a state whose job it is to control and limit the freedom of its citizens. The world that believes in the autonomous free individual also has to believe in the bureaucratic state. Society is seen as a perpetual struggle between these two – sometimes emphasizing the individual, sometimes the collective. But all this is the world of disbelief, the world without God.

This is the world from which Jesus came to redeem us, to give us faith in his Father's love so that we do not need to assert ourselves and our innocence and our rightness, so that we can relax and confess the truth about ourselves, so that we stop judging ourselves and others, because we know that it doesn't matter: God loves us anyway, so that we are liberated enough to risk being vulnerable to others – liberated enough to risk loving and being loved by others, liberated enough to know that we belong to each other because we belong to God. In that world we will not cling fanatically to particular formulas and doctrines simply because they are our security, any more than we cling to our own righteousness. We can be relaxed either way. In such a world a belief that we are called to share in divine life, and do already share in it, can go with a clear awareness of our own weakness and inadequacy and sin. And in such a world believing in God's love can go with a critical awareness of the weakness and inadequacy of our ways of expressing it. Our belief can, and indeed must, go with a certain kind of searching and questioning, a certain kind of doubt. Faith will exclude doubt altogether only when it ceases to be faith and becomes the *vision* of the eternal love which is God.

4

Why God?

When Macbeth hears of the suicide of his wife he gives famous expression to a certain view of life, of history, of the world, in which time becomes simply a mindless succession of events. Time, says Macbeth, is not the time of any story, the development of any plot; tomorrows and yesterdays are nothing but successive moments. It is, he says, an illusion to suppose that there is any story, any tale being enacted. What we think is a story is in the end just like the random mouthings of an idiot, with no connected meaning:

> Tomorrow, and tomorrow, and tomorrow,
> Creeps in this petty pace from day to day,
> To the last syllable of recorded time;
> And all our yesterdays have lighted fools
> The way to dusty death. Out, out, brief candle,
> Life's but a walking shadow, a poor player
> That struts and frets his hour upon the stage,
> And then is heard no more. It is a tale
> Told by an idiot, full of sound and fury
> Signifying nothing.[1]

It seems to me that I can best address the title I have given above by arguing that, without God, Macbeth would be in the end quite right. I say '*in the end* quite right' because I don't

---

[1] William Shakespeare, *Macbeth*, V, v, 19–28.

41

mean that my atheist friends are all living in the kind of despair and disintegration that is represented by Macbeth. I mean only that this seems to me the *logical*, not necessarily the *psychological*, consequence of atheism. Unless our lives are a story told by God they are not a story at all, and this means they have no final meaning.

At one time there was a popular romantic picture of the courageous man who had rejected the props of religion and its illusory comforts, who stood erect on the darkling plain, swept with confused alarms of struggle and fight, facing boldly the fact that life does not provide him with any meaning at all. He is prepared with honesty to manage without it. The difficulty with this alluring picture is that concepts like courage and honesty have to belong to a character in a story, and if in the end there is no story then there is no courage or honesty either. You might as well speak of the honesty and courage and integrity of the warrior ant.

Let me try to explain why I think our lives first of all have to be *given* a meaning, and secondly why they have to be given a meaning *by God*. For it might seem that we can make our own meaning or, if that won't ultimately do, we can be given meaning by our society, culture and history, without recourse to a great storyteller in the sky.

In the first place we are constantly providing meaning for our own actions. That is what we mean by saying that they are deliberate and done for a reason. They are episodes in some coherent story. If you chance to discover me early one morning in your garden in lemon-coloured pyjamas throwing flowerpots through your windows, then, like Lord Emsworth, you may enquire what I am doing, or even 'What is the meaning of this?' And I will tell you a story of which this incident is a part. It finds its place in a story which I am enacting, a story of which I am a character but also the author. In deliberately deciding what I do, I am giving meaning to my behaviour. Doesn't this mean that I provide my own meaning to my life, that I tell my own life-story? Why do I need to drag anyone else in? More especially, why drag God in?

But it will only take you a moment to recognize that you can only tell such stories and provide your actions with such meanings if you are already acting in the context of a whole lot of institutions, a whole lot of frameworks of meaning that are provided for you. There is the language, to start with, in which you formulate your intentions; but, also, gardens, flowerpots and home-ownership (as well as many other things) are all meanings that belong to the society which produced you and in which you formulate aims and purposes and live out your life. There is a larger story, the history of your society and culture, within which you enact your own individual stories. The life which you lead and within which you make deliberate decisions is already a role, or many roles, in institutions that precede you. Your life is to be a character in a story that was begun before you; and if it were not so, if you were not already part of a story, you could not make your own story, decide how to live out your life. And beyond the framework provided for you by your culture, history and language, there is the framework of the animal species to which you belong. This also is a framework of meaning that determines what counts for you as desire and frustration, contentment and revulsion. And it makes possible a story.

That is what I mean by saying that our lives have been given a meaning to start with. We do not start from scratch (as the existentialists used to imagine) to create the meaning of our lives. From the start, our lives are a matter of having a role and a meaning. You were daughters, sons, citizens, Liverpudlians, Christians perhaps, and linguistic, symbol-using animals with particular biological requirements and possibilities, before you ever made one existential choice.

And it is only in the context of these frameworks of meaning that there are any questions to answer, decisions to make, or any life to live. We cannot, then, start from scratch to create the meaning of our lives, although it *does* seem that we could at least try to create an unmeaning, to deny and reject the in-herited frameworks of meaning provided for us by culture and history and nature. And this is exactly what Macbeth is doing in the passage I quoted above.

Matthew Arnold, in an overestimated poem called 'Dover Beach' (where the 'darkling plain' comes from), finding that the world offers him no frame of meaning, 'Nor certitude, nor peace, nor help for pain', cries out, 'Ah, love, let us be true / To one another!' Here, in 'one another', at least we can find some meaning to life. Shakespeare is more ruthless; he has already blocked off this romantic get-out by the suicide of Lady Macbeth. It is just this that provokes Macbeth's speech. He has nobody left to be true to. It is this that convinces him that there is no meaning to time. In the pattern he has tried to impose on time, his wife should have died only after the completion of their reign: 'She should have died hereafter; / There would have been a time for such a word.'[2] By her death, Lady Macbeth is untimely ripped from the pattern – as Macduff (that other omen of disaster) was untimely ripped from his mother's womb. Time is not the time of the intelligible story Macbeth has tried to invent, so for him it has to be just a meaningless succession of days and

> Life's but a walking shadow, a poor player
> That struts and frets his hour upon the stage,
> And then is heard no more. It is a tale
> Told by an idiot, full of sound and fury
> Signifying nothing.

This speech marks the disintegration of Macbeth, indeed his damnation. The audience is confronted with an actor on the stage proclaiming that there is no play, no story, only a petty

---

[2]Ibid., V, v, 17–18.

pace from day to day. He is denying the point of his existence. Macbeth is not merely going to be slain by Macduff within the play, he is seeking to annihilate himself, to opt out of the whole scheme of creation. This actor is not a character in a play. There are no characters. There is no play. There is just sound and fury.

As it seems to me, our lives are to a greater or lesser extent *our own*. They are our own to the extent that we are grown-up, to the extent that we have managed to acquire skills in living (what Aristotle called virtues). To this extent we compose the story of our own lives; we play a part in a drama of our own composition. It marks us off from our fellow-animals that we do not just have a stationary lifetime between birth and death, but a life-*story*, determined by our own decisions – not random choices, but decisions that flow out of our own characters, from what we have made of ourselves. But the decisions we make cannot be made in a vacuum. Our individual life-stories are subplots in a larger story. How our individual subplot fits into the larger story, enriching it or disrupting it and anyway modifying it, is, I suppose, what ethics and moral evaluation is about. Macbeth's subplot starting from the murder of the king has been a story of distortion, of deliberately wrecking the meaning of the larger story, disrupting the custom and usage of his society, and defying what is seen as the order not only of human life but of all animal life and of nature itself. As his subplot crumbles into meaninglessness, Macbeth responds by proclaiming that there is no larger story, it is all an illusion, it is not a story, it is a tale told by an idiot, signifying nothing.

All this is what I mean by saying our lives have been *given* a meaning; there has to be already a story within which and to which we contribute our own stories. That is all very well, perhaps, but why bring *God* into it? Do we need this extra character? Is it not enough that we seek to live our lives in tune with humankind, to tell and enact our own stories within the greater human story, in tune with the appropriate life of our species, in harmony with nature itself?

This is how my humanist atheist friends speak: I mean my grown-up atheist friends, who take seriously the importance of making the best of the only life we have, who want to lead what Socrates or Aristotle would call the good life, who recognize that greed and injustice and cowardice and promiscuity are all things that would diminish them and waste their time, their lifetime. So what has God got to do with it? Isn't God just invented to frighten immature people into behaving themselves because they haven't *seen* that decent human behaviour is valuable in itself? And that's the best case. After all, most gods frighten people into bad and stupid behaviour, into bigotry and cruelty, rather than civilized life in friendship and harmony.

Now I am entirely with my atheist friends in their hostility to the gods. The Jewish tradition from which Christianity comes begins with defiance of the gods; the ten commandments tell us to abandon the gods and live in righteousness, in friendship and justice with each other.

That is fine, but my difficulty with the atheists is this: I cannot see how my life-story can be in tune with humankind, in harmony with my environment and with nature itself, unless my environment and nature itself is musical too. My singing cannot be in harmony, or even out of harmony, with others unless they are singing too. I cannot see how the subplot which is my life can be fitting or even unfitting to the order of nature if that order is not a story too.

My life is *my* own, my *personal* life-story, in so far as I have grown in common sense and practical intelligence, in practical wisdom. This is what makes it a life-story and not just a lifetime. If, then, we are to see the order of nature as a kind of story, then there has to be some kind of intelligence, some kind of wisdom, some kind of a storyteller that makes it a story. There must be some kind of a singer that sings this song. Not, of course, with our particular human, linguistic kind of intelligence and wisdom and singing, but with something analogous to these.

And I want to appropriate the word 'God', take it away from those who believe in the gods, which are indeed illusions and dangerous illusions, and use it to refer to the wisdom by which the world is a story, the singer by which nature is not just sound and fury but music.

What I refer to as God is not any character in the drama of the universe but the author of the universe, the mystery of wisdom which we know of but cannot begin to understand, the wisdom that is the reason why there is a harmony called the universe which we can just stumblingly begin to understand. Our lives are a subplot in the story of the universe, but that story is not one we can comprehend, and it is one that often puzzles us and troubles us and sometimes outrages us. But it is a story. And I say this not because I have *faith*, or *believe* it, but simply because I cannot believe that existence is a tale told by an idiot.

If I were to tell you what I believe, I would tell you much more. I would tell you that by the gift of faith I believe that this story is a love-story, that this song is a love-song, that the wisdom which made this drama so loved his human characters that he became one himself to share their lives; he chose to be a character in the story, to share their hopes and fears and suffering and death.

5

Causes and God

I

When an event surprises us we ask about its cause. When we see the Bishop of Salford rising gently into the air and remaining above our heads without visible means of support, we say, 'I wonder what makes that happen.' If, on the other hand, the bishop remains standing on the ground, we do not ask what causes him to do this. We take it for granted. We ask for causes when we are puzzled and at a loss. I suppose that is why Aristotle, who thought of knowledge as a pursuit of causes, said that it begins with puzzlement or wonder.

It is not merely the unusual that excites our curiosity in this way. The reason why we enquire into the bishop's levitation is not just that it is a rare and unusual event. This can be shown by the following example. A very large number of men are about 5ft 10ins in height, but it is extremely rare to find one who is exactly 5ft $10\frac{1}{3}$ins in height. Although this event is rare, however, we are not surprised by it in the way in which we are surprised by the bishop. What gives its special character to our astonishment with the bishop is not that we don't expect it to happen, but that we expect it *not* to happen. We have more or less definite expectations about the behaviour of things, though we do not always formulate them in words. These expectations are a part of our conception of things. It is not that we constantly have in mind the proposition 'Bishops do not levitate', but a readiness to be surprised at his levitation is part (in an odd way) of understanding the meaning of the word 'bishop'. It is not just that I don't expect the bishop to levitate (someone who has never heard of bishops and does not know the meaning of the word does not expect bishops to levitate). It is a quite positive expectation which could be expressed by saying, 'I expect bishops not to levitate', and I, in some sense, have this thought even though I do not say it out loud or even to myself.

II

Expectations about the behaviour of things I shall call knowledge of their nature. For when something behaves in an expected way we say, 'Well naturally it does that.' And it is to be noticed that causes and nature are in some way opposed. When something is natural we don't think it needs a cause. If someone drinks a glass of beer and suddenly writhes in agony and falls to the ground foaming at the mouth, I can start investigating the cause of this. I say, 'What caused that?' But if the person in question simply looks a little more cheerful, I don't puzzle about causes, and if I did say, 'What causes that to happen?', people would answer, 'Nothing. Why shouldn't it happen? It's perfectly natural.'

The surprising situation in which we ask about causes is one in which things seem to be behaving unnaturally. We are not puzzled when a dog runs about or when a tree stands stock-still for days. It is when the tree moves about and the dog stands stock-still that we begin to enquire. Now what is this enquiry? What are we looking for? What will count as success in it? This is a question that, it seems to me, has not engaged philosophers enough. I think the answer to it is that we think the enquiry has succeeded when we can say, 'Ah, now I see that it was all perfectly natural after all.' The enquiry begins when we find what seems to be *unnatural* behaviour, and it ends when we recognize it as *natural* behaviour, as what might have been expected if we'd only known. Ideally the enquiry into the behaviour of the bishop should end not merely with the conclusion that because of these and these hitherto unnoticed factors it was quite natural for him to be floating in the air, but also with the conclusion that it would have been unnatural for him *not* to have been.

In passing I ought to qualify this by saying that it is not universally the case that if to do A is natural, then not to do A is unnatural. It depends on how A is described. If 'doing A' is a description purely in terms of, say, physical movements, then we might want to say that doing A and not doing A are both equally natural to an animal. It is the characteristic feature of living things that their natural behaviour has to be described at a higher level of language than that of physical movement. Thus there are many different and contradictory physical-movement descriptions which could count as examples of the natural activities of animals – such as eating, or hunting, or searching. The fact that the natural behaviour of living things has to be described in such words of a relatively higher logical level is what is meant by saying that they have souls. But this is a digression.

The notion of cause, therefore, seems to depend on the notion of nature and the natural. The question 'What is the cause of this?' is to be construed as 'In what way can this be seen as quite natural?' We can stylize the picture like this. You have, it seems, A and B, and you know what is natural for them (you know what you can expect them to do), but it turns out that something quite different is happening. You are surprised and look for the cause, and you discover that besides A and B you also have C, D and E, and when you consider the behaviour that is natural to C, D and E, you realize that the grouping ABCDE will quite naturally produce the thing that surprised you at first.

What have you discovered? You have formulated more precisely the natural behaviour of some things. Perhaps in some

cases you have formulated for the first time what has been hitherto a merely inarticulate expectation. This is what finding a
cause means. It means seeing how such and such is, after all,
quite natural.

Of course, there is no such thing as naturalness in general.
There is no such thing as natural behaviour as such. There is
only behaviour which is natural to this or that kind of thing.
One cannot recognize this or that as natural activities unless
one recognizes the thing which has the activity. It is for this
reason that looking for the cause comes to mean looking for
the *thing* which is the cause. Of course, an account of the cause
usually involves referring to *many things* interacting.

III

One cannot ask, 'What is the cause of *this?*' and merely point.
It is impossible to make sense of the question 'What is the cause
of...?' unless some description of the effect is either formulated
or implied. By a description being implied I mean this: if the
bishop rose into the air, I *could* say, 'What is the cause of this?'
because it would be clear from the context that 'this' referred
to the bishop rising into the air. There is a cause of George
being ill, or of Germany *being defeated*, or of the train *being
late*, or the bishop *rising*. One cannot point to an effect any
more than one can point to the meaning of a word; both are
what medieval philosophers would have called 'formal'. One
cannot point to a form. Forms are not identified by pointing.
They are identified by language. You can point to George, but
not to the being-ill of George; this can only be described. I
think this is what the medievals meant by saying that forms
are intellectually apprehended.

There are of course an indefinite number of things exercising
their natural activity in relation to George, but only some of

these are relevant to the being ill of George. When we seek the cause of his illness we seek just these.

IV

Of course the word 'thing' here is deliberately vague. I shall not try here to make it more precise, but I do think that before proceeding on I ought to say a little more about what I mean by *natural* activity.

When we say that some behaviour is natural to A, we mean that given the sort of thing that A is, this is what you would expect. Naturalness, in fact, is governed not by the particular individual but by the kind of thing that the individual is. This is the *first* point.

The *second* is that it is not merely a contingent fact that *this* kind of thing acts naturally in *this* way. When we say that such and such is natural activity for this kind of thing we are claiming to see a connection between the thing and its activity. Our expectations about the activity of the thing are in some way intelligibly connected with our understanding of what it is. We are claiming (perhaps falsely in some cases) that there is more to it than the simple fact that we have been conditioned to expect *this* activity from *this* kind of thing.

The *third* point is that things do not *always* act naturally. The cases when they fail to do so are those in which we are surprised and seek for causes. The fact is that the natural behaviour of a thing is what it mostly does. It is what it does, to use St Thomas's phrase, *ut in pluribus*, for the most part.[1] We take chunks of potassium nitrate out of the bottle and they all do the same kind of things, and then we come across a chunk which behaves differently. We are surprised, but we do *not* say, 'It is

[1] See, for example, *Summa Contra Gentiles*, III, 38.

not logically possible that this should be potassium nitrate, for nothing counts as KNO_3 unless it does all these things.' This kind of thing happens all the time, and we may think that the exception is worth investigating, or again we may just chuck it away. It is no good saying here: 'But all that this means is that your unusual sample of potassium nitrate contained some impurities. Pure potassium nitrate always behaves in exactly the same way.' It is no good saying this because, of course, pure KNO_3 is a theoretical construct. All samples of potassium nitrate contain impurities. I am speaking of the way in which the language is actually used. When we say to the lab assistants, 'Fetch me some potassium nitrate', they bring what is in the bottle.

The fact that *ut in pluribus* statements can have logical necessity was one of Wittgenstein's most interesting doctrines. He pointed out that it is not merely a contingent fact, but a logically necessary one, that *most*, though not all, laws are obeyed, and *most*, though not all, statements are understood. There can be a certain amount of disobedience, and a certain amount of misunderstanding, but the existence of law or language depends on this being below a certain minimum. A similar necessity attaches to the *ut in pluribus* statements about natural activities and natural properties. There can be a certain number of imbeciles and a certain number of men who are paralysed, but men exist at all because *most* men are not like this. So we say that it is not natural to a man to be an imbecile or paralysed. Again I must emphasize that it is not just their rarity which makes them unnatural, but the fact that it is necessary that they should be rare. Unnatural conditions are conditions that can only exist by being exceptional. Forgery and cancer are examples of this. Too many forged notes will destroy a currency and thereby destroy the forged ones as well. Too much cancer will destroy the body and thereby the cancer as well.

This, I believe, is the distinction to be drawn, for an Aristotelian, between the essence of a thing and its properties. The essence of a thing is what it takes for the thing to be at all. The ascription of essence is always tautological. It would be self-contradictory to say of human beings that they are not animals. The essence has to do with the existence of something, the properties with its existence within a *world*. If there is to be a possible world containing sparrows, then *most* sparrows must be able to fly most of the time. Being able to fly is a property of sparrows. A sparrow unable to fly is a deficient or bad sparrow. A bad sparrow is one of the minority which has the essence of a sparrow but lacks some property. The properties of a thing are what is natural to it.

V

When we investigate a cause, then, we are looking for the natural activities which will produce a formal effect. When George is ill we seek the things whose natural behaviour in this circumstance *is* the being ill of George. What we do is reinterpret the situation. At the moment in our description (e.g. 'George is being sick on the carpet'), the subjects have not, so to speak, got their natural predicates. It is not natural to George to be sick on the carpet. How then can we redescribe what we have seen so that each actor (the germs, the alcohol, George, etc.) have each got their natural role? When we have done this work we have given the cause.

The work of finding causes is simply a work of redescription. Of course this is not an armchair activity (especially if George is in the armchair). It may involve any amount of scientific experiment and probing into things. But its ultimate purpose is to find a language in which the event can be described with predicates which are natural to their subjects – or, as Aristotle would say, with 'proper predicates'. And if anyone asks, 'In what way is your new description superior to the old one?' – for, after all, they both describe exactly the same thing – the only answer is that the second one is more satisfactory because it shows us how we can say 'of course' or 'naturally'.

VI

The kindness of people may be exhibited in a number of different ways. They may listen patiently to the boring conversation of the elderly, or they may give money to beggars, or they may take great care to avoid snubbing others. All these are things that look quite different, but they are all ways in which what we think of as the single characteristic of kindness is at work. The concept of kindness is such that confronted with such quite diverse activities we can say, 'She gives money to beggars, so *naturally* she tries not to snub people.'

It is a great part of the business of a scientific investigation to achieve formulations of natural activities which will thus unify a whole range of what, at first sight, seem quite different events. We should like to be able to say, 'If you throw water on the fire, it puts it out, so *naturally* if you throw it onto sodium it bursts into flames.' In the chemical analysis of water, etc. we have a formulation which precisely enables us to say this. We try all the time to pass from the anecdotal phase, in which we mention the various things that happen to water, to the scientific phase, in which we can see all this as merely a matter of water exerting itself in different circumstances. We begin by seeing cause and effect as separate, but our aim is to reinterpret the effect as nothing but the active presence of the cause.

In other words, there is, it seems to me, no such thing as causality which causes exert, and we will get nowhere if we try to conceive of a single action (for example a sort of pushing) which is what causes do. Causes are just things exerting *themselves* naturally, and what is natural for one thing is of course quite different from what is natural for another.

My thesis throughout so far has been that causal explanation only exists because things have characteristic natural behaviour. To put it as simply as possible, each sort of thing has just one sort of effect. Now, of course, this effect may look very different in different circumstances, as we saw in the case of human kindness. But these are all just different shapes which the same effectiveness takes on in different surroundings. In all cases what you have is simply the cause exerting itself.

VII

I have been speaking throughout this essay of causal *explanation*. I have pretended to assume that what makes us seek the cause is the desire for an explanation. But, of course, there may be other reasons for seeking the cause – notably the desire to control events. Your may want to know the cause of George being sick in order to *stop him* being sick or in order to *make him* sick. You might call this the technologist's interest as opposed to the scientist's interest. Of course it is usually the technological interest which stimulates and makes possible the scientific investigation, but the technologist as such can stop short of the scientific ideal.

Provided that he knows what he has to do with the materials to hand in order to produce a certain effect, he is satisfied. He is not (precisely as a technologist) interested in the scientist's job of redescription and analysis, the purpose of which is to see the effect as natural and inevitable. The technologist as such does not care why it works so long as it works. Of course I do not mean that anyone could be a technologist without also being a scientist. But the jobs are different. One wants to *do*, the other wants to *see*. A great many of the uses of the word 'cause' in our language are based on this technological sense. A cause is roughly whatever we have to do to bring about an effect. It is in this sense that we say that the pressing of a switch causes the light to go on, or that going out without a coat causes a cold, or that a cracked rivet caused the aircraft to crash. It is clear that these causes are not explanatory causes. It is only in an unmentioned but recognized context of other things that they can be called explanations. They are only called causes because they are picked on as the most easily controlled factor in the situation.

VIII

At this point perhaps I might be allowed to point out that for St Thomas Aquinas, a *causa efficiens* or *agens* (efficient or agent cause) was an explanatory cause in the full sense. Other things or events can only be called *causae* (causes) by a figure of speech. They are *causae per accidens* (causes in a manner of speaking). They are not called causes because of what they are, or because of their natural behaviour, but only because they happen to be involved in some way in the causal activity of something else.

Much of what Aquinas says about causes is only intelligible if we recognize that he means *causa* (cause) in its full sense. When we recognize this, statements which at first sight seem wildly incredible become the illuminating platitudes of which metaphysics consists. If we want to say that the cracked rivet was the cause of the air disaster, then no sense at all can be made of the idea that causes produce effects similar to themselves. In what respect does an electric light resemble a pressed switch? If, however, we take 'cause' in its restricted sense of explanatory cause these ideas are simple enough. I have said that the cause, in this sense, is the thing of which the natural activity is the effect, i.e. the effect is what it is like when the cause exerts *itself*. Each kind of thing has only one effect, though this effect may, as we have seen, take different shapes in different circumstances. This exertion of itself on the part of the cause is spoken of by St Thomas as the production of a similitude of itself (*omne agens agit sibi simile*), and it is for this reason that we can speak of knowing a cause in its effects.[2]

Of course if we are to know a cause in its effect we must be able to disentangle the characteristic effect of the cause from the shape which has been given to it by its circumstances. In fact, seeking the cause in the effect is nothing but this work of distentangling. When we have isolated the precise formal effect of the cause then we know the cause.

What I have called 'disentanglement' is of course a process of redescription. For since, as I have suggested, effects are formal, and forms can only be identified by language, two different descriptions are in fact descriptions of different effects. When we get the right descriptions we have seen the right effect and we know the cause.

Let me take a simple example. When someone speaks, a description of the occurrence can be given simply in terms of sound, vibrations of various frequencies in the air. Or alternatively, a fuller description can be given which takes account of the significant character of the sounds. These are two alternative descriptions of the same thing (if a piece of speech can be regarded as a thing), but they are not two alternative descriptions of the same effect; they are descriptions of two different effects. Whether or not we see the cause in the piece of speech which is produced will depend on whether or not we recognize it as the effect that it is, and do not mistake it for another. Thus, the sounds produced by a parrot might be mistaken for speech, as the sounds produced by a jackal might be mistaken for laughter. If we make this mistake we mistake parrots and jackals for human beings, since speech and laughter are the result of human beings exerting themselves. In a similar way, if we look at human speech simply in terms of sounds, without regard to significance, we are looking at an effect which is not

---

[2]See, for example, *Summa Contra Gentiles*, II, 23.

produced by the human being *qua* human being. It is an effect which, in St Thomas's language, is not *adequate* to the cause producing it.

IX

This, I think, is of interest because St Thomas thought that God can be called a cause of the world, but he explained the fact that we do not know God from the world by the fact that the world is an inadequate effect of this cause. Now it might seem at first sight that this means that the world is an effect which *could have* been produced by something other than God and only *happens* to have been produced by God – just as the vibrations in the air could have been the effect of a parrot and only happen to be the effect of a human being. But it seems unlikely that he meant this. What he meant can perhaps be made clear by going back to the parrot. Suppose, *per impossibile*, that there are people who have no idea of what is meant by significance. They do not understand what speech is, as distinct from sounds in the air. They cannot in any way explain the difference between a voice and a noise. Such people, of course, would be unaware of the *human* (that is why I said *per impossibile*). On hearing speech they would see it as the effect of the movements of tongues and teeth and things. Now suppose that they in some way become aware that when certain animals produce sounds there is more to it than simply the vibrations of the air (although of course they cannot say *what* this more is). Then they will say that the vibrations are an adequate effect of the larynx, and so on, but an inadequate effect of some higher cause which imports this mysterious other formality into them. If they could only grasp the concept of significance, then they would be able to so redescribe the vibrations as to say, 'This is the adequate effect of a human being', and then of course they would grasp the concept of the human. What makes it impossible for them to see the cause in the effect, what makes the effect an inadequate one for them, is their inability to re-describe it.

X

We think of God as though he were a cause, i.e. a thing which has a natural behaviour, a thing which exerts itself. In exerting itself it produces a characteristic effect. But in the case of God we want to say that his characteristic effect is the 'to be' of things. The thing that we find in common to all effects of God is that they exist. Now just as we can go back from characteristic effect to the nature of the cause in other cases (we can say such and such is the characteristic effect of a cause with a human nature, a cause to which it is natural to act humanly, this on the other hand is the characteristic effect of a cause with a canine nature), so we can say the same of God. If the characteristic effect of a thing is human we say that its nature is to be human. With God we say that his characteristic effect is the 'to be' of things, and so his nature is to be. A cause with a human nature humanizes things; a cause with a divine nature makes them exist.

The trouble with all this is that it is entirely a matter of words. It is one thing to *say* that what all the effects of God have in common is that they exist, and quite another thing to conceive what this means. While we can disentangle or abstract a common element which all effects of a particular created cause may have, no sense can be made of disentangling or abstracting the common element of existence. Existence, in spite of being an abstract noun, is not a common element of the things that exist. It does not name something which every existing thing has. It is one thing for a tree to exist and quite another thing for white-ness to exist and another thing for a man to exist. To say that a man exists is just to say that he is a man. To say that whiteness exists it just to say that something is white. And, clearly, these are quite different statements.

I have suggested that effects are always formal. It is the being-ill of Fido (the dog), or the being defeated of Germany, that is caused. But clearly whatever we mean by the existence of Fido is not a formal characteristic of him. As a matter of fact, Fido can be made to exist by a cause, but not by inducing existence into something, only by inducing some formal effects which result in his 'caninity' or 'dogness'. If you can make something into a dog, then, of course, you make it into an existent dog. But the word 'existent' does not enter into your description of the formal effect of the cause. You just say, 'It's a dog.' If it could and did, you would be speaking of a different effect of a different cause (for, as I have said, you cannot have two different descriptions of the same effect). In fact when we say that God is a cause we are saying that it is as though the word 'existent' could and does enter into the description of things. It is as though to exist *were* a characteristic of things. It is as though we can class things as existent as opposed to non-existent in the way in which we can class them as human as opposed to non-human.

XI

Now of course we cannot really do this. I only say *as though* we could do it. On this point there is a wide and interesting divergence between the views of St Thomas Aquinas and those of the later scholastic philosophers who are frequently supposed to be his followers. He himself was not completely opposed to metaphysics. He did not think it was absolute *nonsense* to speak of the *esse* (the 'to be') of things, even though he was well aware that we have no single concept of being, even though he recognized that what it is for things to be depends entirely on what they are. He insisted that 'beings' is not a class-name, that there is no class of beings over against a class of nonbeings. All the same, though, he thought that we could speak (metaphysically) of the 'to be' of things. His reason for this was not that our concept of anything included the concept of existence, but that when we use our concepts in the assertion of statements we make an implicit appeal to something beyond the conceptual. To state that the cat is on the mat is to do something more than to understand the meanings of the words involved. It is to have truth (or perhaps falsity) in mind. What it is for a statement to be true can never be completely analysed in conceptual terms. To have a concept is, of course for St Thomas, to know how to use a word and 'knowing *that*' can never be reduced to 'knowing *how*'. He constantly insists on the difference between the two 'acts of the mind', between understanding the meaning of a word and making a statement, and it is in the latter only that we attain *esse* (the 'to be' of things), not by any kind of abstraction or conceptualization. Briefly, St Thomas thought that while it is possible to discuss questions of meaning without bringing in the word 'existence', it is needed in order to distinguish questions of meaning from questions of truth and falsity. And 'existence' does this job precisely by *not* being just another concept. In other words, Aquinas claims that the existence of things can be intellectually grasped even though we have no concept of it. As Wittgenstein might have observed, it can be shown but not said.[3]

XII

In this Aquinas differs radically from many of the later scholastics. The difference can best be seen by looking at two contrasting formulations of an argument for the existence of God.

---

[3]Cf. Ludwig Wittgenstein, *Tractatus Logico-Philosophicus*, 6.5–522.

For the later view, which I shall call 'the metaphysics of contingency', there is supposed to be an argument for God's existence on these lines:

Everything we come across that exists is capable of not existing, for we can imagine that anything we know of does not exist, and such beings are known as contingent beings. There must therefore be a reason why they exist rather than not existing, and this reason is God, who is not a contingent but a necessary being.

We can contrast this argument, which is sometimes called 'the cosmological argument', with the third way of showing that God exists as found in Aquinas's *Summa Theologiae*, Ia, 2, 3. In fact, it derives from a misunderstanding of this third way.

First of all, notice that 'the cosmological argument' supposes that we can think of things either as existing or not existing. But this St Thomas would deny. You cannot, for him, think of something as not existing. Existence is not a form or characteristic. For a thing to exist is for it to have its essence. So there cannot be a nonexistent essence. If something ceases to exist you are not left with an essence lacking existence. You are left with a meaningful noun which is not the name of anything.

St Thomas's own argument, which is caricatured in the cosmological argument, begins not with the idea that we can conceive of things as not existing but with the fact that a lot of things are perishable. They rot away or get destroyed one way or another. These are the contingent things. Their existence is contingent upon certain causes. What makes them exist rather than not exist are the causes which bring them into existence – various natural causes.

Now St Thomas claims to be able to show that not everything in the world can be like this, that we have to postulate some non-contingent necessary things. He located these necessary beings in the heavens (the stars, and so on). Whatever we may think of his argument at this point (personally I think there is a mistake in logic) there does seem to be a tendency for scientific explanation to seek out necessary beings to explain the goings-on of perishable things. Nowadays instead of looking for them in astronomy we look for them in the subatomic world. Finally St Thomas asks whether the very necessity of these necessary beings does not raise a question.

His argument is, as he says, not from the contingency of things but from *possibili et necessario* (the possible and the necessary). He says first of all that there are necessary things as well as contingent things. Now, why this difference? Why aren't the necessary things like the contingent ones? How can they be that way? It is the capacity of the necessary beings to account for the contingent ones that needs to be accounted for. How is it that these beings (being necessary) are able so successfully and adequately to account for other things?

XIII

This is the major difference between St Thomas's views and what is sometimes called 'the metaphysics of contingency'. For the latter we invoke God as the stable background, the necessary being which lies behind the mutability of things. For this view creaturehood essentially consists in being contingent, in requiring explanation. For St Thomas, on the other hand, the job which metaphysicians of contingency assign to God is to be assigned to scientific explanation. Behind the mutability of things lies the order of nature. Events in the world are to be explained, and completely and adequately explained, by natural causes. It is only when we have said this that we come to God.

For Aquinas, God is required as the reason why natural causes really do of themselves cause. We need to account for the fact that the world is self-explanatory. St Thomas does not drag God in because scientific explanations are unsatisfactory and inadequate. He brings them in because they are satisfactory. And why should this be puzzling? Because when we have finished saying that such and such is indeed the adequate and appropriate effect of such and such a cause, there remains the fact that in giving this nature, this formal effect, to a thing the cause has really brought something into *being*. The metaphysics of contingency sees 'being' as a characteristic to be accounted for, more or less as other characteristics are accounted for. For this we need God. God is doing the same kind of job as any other cause except that what he supplies is being. Without God there would be nothing, just as without other causes things would lack other characteristics.

This tendency to regard God as working alongside, or doing the same kind of job as, other causes has effects in a lot of other philosophical and theological fields. For St Thomas, God as creator makes no difference to the world, for to exist is not to be different from not existing. All differences are formal and can be adequately accounted for by created causes.

The metaphysics of contingency argues that since all things are contingent there must be something behind them which brings them out of nothing. There must be a God as well as creatures, because it is not conceivable that from *nothing* there should have emerged the existing world. There must therefore have been not nothing, but *God* prior to the world. Against this, some philosophers have argued that there is no need for a God because it is quite conceivable that the world should have emerged from nothing. Why shouldn't it?

Aquinas has a third position to offer. He argues that it is utterly inconceivable that the world should have emerged from nothing, but he adds that nevertheless this is precisely what happened. He does not feel constrained to postulate God and creation because he finds the notion of nothing pre-existing the world repugnant to his mind. On the contrary, his view is that, in so far as we can picture creation at all, that is how we must picture it. For St Thomas, God is not invoked to fill in any gap left by the absence of anything else. He does not do any job that other causes might do. To say that God created the world is in no way to eliminate the intellectual vertigo we feel when we try to think of the beginning of things. Recognition of God's action does not remove any of the mystery from the world.

6

On Evil and Omnipotence

I The problem

I was provoked into writing this paper by rereading a most interesting article by Professor Antony Flew called 'Divine Omnipotence and Human Freedom'.[1] I am ashamed to say that it was only on a fifth or sixth reading that I noticed the significance of one particular remark: 'the Roman Catholic account of the universe and its Creator would surely gain rather than lose in plausibility if it were presented as far as possible "aseptically"; in language stripped of all terms of favourable and unfavourable appraisal'.[2]

This remark suggests that there is a considerable danger of agreement between Professor Flew and the Roman Catholic theologian. For of course, to the Roman Catholic, or to anyone of any religion at all, the idea of making a 'favourable appraisal' of God is simply ludicrous. However, there is no need to fear. Professor Flew, indeed, does seem to me to come to several correct conclusions, but since he also seems to me to come there for bad reasons the disagreement is safe.

He begins with the following statement of the problem of evil: 'Either God cannot abolish evil or he will not; if he cannot then he is not all-powerful; if he will not then he is not

---

[1] Antony Flew, 'Divine Omnipotence and Human Freedom', in Antony Flew and Alasdair MacIntyre (eds), *New Essays in Philosophical Theology* (London: SCM Press, 1955), pp. 144–69.
[2] Ibid., p. 159.

all-good.'[3] Professor Flew's purpose is to examine what he calls the 'Free-will Defence'. Briefly, this is that God could not make people free without there being the possibility that they would choose evil, and the evil in the world is in some way connected with their sin. There is also a subsidiary strand of the Defence: that certain goods and virtues, such as forgiveness and tolerance, demand for their exercise the actual occurrence of moral evil. I shall not consider this subsidiary argument in what follows.

Professor Flew's move against the Free-will Defence is to question 'the idea that there is a contradiction involved in saying that God might have made people so that they always in fact *freely* chose the right'.[4] If there is no contradiction here, says Flew, then 'Omnipotence might have made a world inhabited by wholly virtuous people; the Free-will Defence is broken-backed.'[5] Flew thinks that God could have made a world in which by arrangement everyone freely chose to do good, and the reason for this, he thinks, is that freedom is not incompatible with determinism. A human action, he thinks, can be both caused and free.

I want to try to convince you of two propositions. The first is that Professor Flew is entirely right in supposing the Free-will Defence to be worthless, though his reasons for thinking this are bad ones. The second is that although God could have made a world in which everyone freely chose good, and although he manifestly did not do so, this does not in any way detract from his infinite goodness.

II The Free-will Defence and Professor Flew's case

It might be thought that since Professor Flew and I are in agreement about the Free-will Defence we might just as well take that

[3]Ibid., p. 144.
[4]Ibid., p. 149.
[5]Ibid.

as read and pass on to the bits where we disagree. I shall not do this because I want to explain *my* reasons for rejecting the Free-will Defence. I want to do this not merely for the sake of being different from Professor Flew, but because the explanation may throw some light on the notions of omnipotence and creation, notions we shall need to be clear about later in this paper. I do not want to spend a lot of time criticizing Professor Flew's reasons, since if I were to do them justice it would take more time than I have now. Very briefly, I should argue that the proposition that human acts are causally determined does not follow either from the fact that they can be predictable, or from the fact that they have causal conditions, or from the fact that they are motivated.

Of course, George can predict on Friday that Fred will go freely to the football match on Saturday. We can have reasonable expectations about his free actions as we can about his unfree actions. We can be reasonably sure that if he is left alone with his grandmother he will not murder her, just as we can be reasonably sure that if he is pushed off a cliff he will hit the rocks below. We are not a hundred per cent sure in either case, of course; but it is impossible to be a hundred per cent sure of any contingent fact. An important difference between free and unfree acts is brought out by considering our reactions when our predictions turn out wrong. When our expectations about Fred's unfree acts are disappointed we look for some cause which interfered with him. He didn't hit the rocks because a helicopter intercepted him, or his braces got caught on a tree. When our expectations about his free acts are disappointed we do not immediately suppose that there *must* be a cause that interfered. Instead, we may ask why he changed his mind, what reason or motive he had. Sometimes we think that what he took as a motive was unreasonable, in which case we blame him; sometimes we think it was reasonable; but in either case we think that he *took* such and such as a motive. This is what we do in a free action – we make something our motive for acting. Of itself it does not have to be a motive. We make it such for ourselves. We cannot predict with a hundred per cent certainty that Fred will always take this or that as his motive, but knowing about Fred partly means knowing about the things that he is disposed to take as motives: knowing, that is, about his virtues and vices and dispositions.

So, a person's free actions are not random, in the sense of indeterminate. They are determined by motives and reasons. But people decide for themselves what will count with them for a motive. Freedom means determining yourself. When we are surprised by an unfree act we revise our view of the causal set-up; when we are surprised by a free act we revise our view of the person whose act it is. We may look for causes too, but only in so far as we regard the action as unfree. Prediction of Fred's acts by means of knowledge of his dispositions and virtues is qualified by the fact that we are always prepared to change our estimation of him. We are prepared for him to act out of character not because we have previously misread his character but simply because he has changed. When a machine goes wrong, we are surprised, interested and puzzled; and we look for the interfering cause. When a hitherto honest man embezzles the funds, we are shocked as well as surprised – i.e. our estimate of the man changes, and we look for causes (mental breakdown, etc.) in so far as we do not think he could help it. It does not seem to me that in his article Professor Flew pays sufficient attention to the cases in which we feel the need to revise our estimate of people, and it is this which leads him *from* the fact that free actions are usually predictable *to* the implausible view that they are predictable in the same way as caused acts.

III The Free-will Defence and the Thomist case

I do not know whether you are with me in these very hasty criticisms of Professor Flew's argument that free acts can be determined beforehand, but, whether he is right about this or not, it seems to me that he is certainly right in concluding that the Free-will Defence is broken-backed. This, however, is not because free acts are determined in the same way as other happenings in the world, but because they are determined directly by God. Unlike Professor Flew, I see a contradiction between freedom and determinism, but I see no contradiction between freedom and predestination. The Free-will Defence is based on the idea that freedom makes us independent of God, and I want to claim that whether or not Professor Flew is right in saying that freedom doesn't even make us independent of other creatures, it certainly doesn't make us independent of God.

My task therefore is first to show how freedom can be compatible with complete dependence on God and, secondly, having destroyed the Free-will Defence, to show how evil and sin are compatible with the goodness of God.

Can omnipotence limit itself?

What do we mean by omnipotence? When we say that God is omnipotent we mean that any situation that can be described coherently could be brought about by God. This rules out logical impossibilities, square circles and the like.

Now it might be thought that God's omnipotence implies merely that he *could* control everything that happens – not that he *does* in fact so control it. It might be thought that our free actions are acts that God chooses not to control. Even if God is able to do everything, it does not follow that he does do everything. But this is an error. It is certainly the case that, although God can do anything, there must be nothing that he is not able to do. Now if freedom means being independent of God's control, and if there were free creatures, it would follow that there were activities, the activities of these creatures, which God was *unable* to control, and this *would* be a limitation on his omnipotence. Some have thought that God's omnipotence is limited in this way. They hold that free acts are not due to God though he knows beforehand what I am going to do with my freedom. Being outside time he sees past, present and future in one vision, and so is able to predict with certainty what I will do, even though he does not control it. According to one version of this theory, God can plan his world in view of what he foresees we will make of it. (Associated with this theory is the notion of *scientia media*, for which, I was astonished to see, Professor Flew has some kind words in a footnote.[6] Of this I will say nothing at present except that it seems to me to possess the unique merit of denying simultaneously *both* divine omnipotence *and* human freedom.)

J. L. Mackie has criticized this notion of an omnipotence that limits itself. He writes:

> This leads us to what I call the Paradox of Omnipotence: can an omnipotent being make things which he cannot subsequently control? It is clear that this is a paradox: the question cannot be answered satisfactorily either in the affirmative or in the negative. If we answer 'Yes', it follows that if God actually makes things which he cannot control, or makes rules which bind himself, he is not omnipotent once he has made them: there are *then* things which he cannot do. But if we answer 'No', we are immediately asserting that there are things which he cannot do, that is to say that he is already not omnipotent.[7]

Mackie resolves his paradox by invoking the notions of 'first- and second-order omnipotence', but I cannot see that we have here a paradox at all. The answer is to be simply 'No'. God

[6] Ibid., p. 156 n. 18.
[7] J. L. Mackie, 'Evil and Omnipotence' (1955), repr. in Marilyn McCord Adams and Robert Merrihew Adams (eds), *The Problem of Evil* (Oxford: Oxford University Press, 1990), pp. 34–5.

cannot make things that he subsequently cannot control. The inability to do so is no limitation upon omnipotence since what is in question is a logical impossibility. The phrase 'creature outside the control of an omnipotent God' is self-cancelling, like the phrase 'square circle'.

It seems to me, therefore, that the omnipotence of God plainly means that everything that actually happens is due to God. As we shall be seeing later, it is important to notice that phrase 'everything that actually happens'. We cannot in the same sense say that when something doesn't happen its not happening is brought about by God. We cannot sensibly say that God has brought it about that there is not a pink giraffe in the room. He has simply failed to bring it about that there is a pink giraffe in the room.

Quite a lot of what actually happens is freely done by people, so our first problem is to reconcile the two propositions 'This action was freely done by Peter' and 'This action was caused by God'. I am not able here to fall back on Professor Flew's defence that freedom is compatible with causal determinism, for I hold that freedom and determination by outside causes are mutually exclusive. In so far as an act is due to me (i.e. is free), it is not due to other causes. In so far as it is due to other causes, it is not due to me, and hence not free. I shall argue, however, that freedom and causal determination by God are not incompatible because God's causality is unique. He is not an outside cause in the sense that other creatures are.

The uniqueness of God's causality

It is with God's activity as it is with his presence. He does not take up space. If I fill up a basket with apples and oranges, the more apples there are, the less room there is for oranges, and vice versa. The apples and the oranges compete for the available space. But apples and God do not compete for available space.

We can say that God is everywhere, that there is no such thing as a place where he is not, for wherever there is anything God is there holding it in being. God is not, of course, himself spatial. He has no size or position or shape. But we can nevertheless say that he is present everywhere. Clearly he is not *alongside* his creatures. We do not say that the more apples there are in the basket the less room there is for God. The apples do not have to shift over to make room for God. The presence of God does not leave less room for the apples. On the contrary, it is because of the presence of God that the apples are there at all. We can say, 'There is nothing here except an apple', just *because* God is there too. The apple is not moved to one side by God. It is where it is because of God.

Now it is the same with causality as with spatial presence. Created causes compete with each other. This activity is due to me and to that extent it is not due to causes other than me. Usually an activity is due partly to me and partly to other causes. The other causes make a difference to my activity. My activity is like *this*, though it would have been like *that* but for the interference of some other causes. That is how we detect the operation of other causes. The more the other causes operate, the less the activity is due to me; the less responsible I am for it, the less it is a free action.

But the activity of God does not make any *difference* to my activity. It makes it what it is in the first place. It is because of the activity of the Creator that I have *my own* activity to begin with. God is not alongside me, competing with me, an alternative to me, taking up space that I could have occupied or doing things that I might have done.

Creation and 'making a difference'

All created causes make a difference to the world. They are parts of the world which impose themselves on other parts of the world. When the hurricane has passed by, you can see that a hurricane has passed by; the world is different from what it was before. But God's creative and sustaining activity does not make the world different from what it is – how could it? It makes the world what it is. The specific characteristic effect of the Creator is that things should exist, just as the specific characteristic effect of a kicker is that things should be kicked. But clearly there is no difference between existing and not existing. The world is not changed in any way by being created. If you like, you can talk about the horse before it began to exist and the horse after it began to exist (though it is an odd way of talking); but you must not say that there is any difference between the two, for if the horse before it began to exist was different, then a different horse would have come into existence.

A hurricane leaves its thumbprint on the world, but God does not leave any such thumbprint. We can say, 'This looks as though a hurricane has been here', but we cannot sensibly say, 'This looks as though God has been here.' That is why the famous 'Argument from Design' (commonly attributed to William Paley) is a silly one.[8] You can't say, 'Look how the world is [orderly, complicated or whatever], so it must have been made by God.' You can no more say, 'This sort of world must have been made by God', than you can say, 'This sort of world must exist.' The arguments of St Thomas Aquinas to show that God exists (as distinct from the five arguments usually attributed to him) do not try to show that because the world has this or that feature it must be made by God. They try to lead us from consideration of this or that feature to the very difficult and elusive metaphysical notion that the world exists instead of not existing.

God's activity, then, does not compete with mine. Whereas the activity of any other creature makes a difference to mine and would interfere with my freedom, the activity of God makes

---

[8]For Paley's argument, see William Paley, *Natural Theology* (1802), Chs 1–3.

no difference. It has a more fundamental and important job to do than making a difference. It makes me have my own activity in the first place. I am free; I have my own spontaneous activity not determined by other creatures, because God makes me free. Not free of him (this would be to cease to exist), but free of other creatures.

The idea that God's causality could interfere with my freedom can only arise from an idolatrous notion of God as a very large and powerful creature – a part of the world. We see an ascending scale of powerful causes. The more powerful the cause, the more difference it makes. And we are inclined to locate God at the top of the scale, and to imagine that he makes the most difference of all. But God does not make the most difference. He makes, if you like, *all* the difference – which is the same as making no difference at all. So far as the kind of world we have is concerned, the atheist and the theist will expect to see exactly the same features. The only difference is that if the atheist were right, the question would not arise – indeed, the atheist would not arise.

Redemption and making a difference

Perhaps I should explain here that the atheist and the *Christian* would have very different expectations. For the Christian is not merely a theist – i.e. not merely one who is convinced that the world is created by an omnipotent God. Christians also believe that, besides creating the world, God has *also* intervened and made a difference to it *as well*. I believe that when our minds are enlightened by the gift of faith we can see the marks of this divine intervention in history. But all this is quite irrelevant to philosophy, which is wholly concerned with the things we can know without faith. The fact that people are not theists does not by any means mean that they are Christian.

It merely means that one barrier to their being Christians is removed.

The activity of God, then, is not an alternative to my free activity. It is its source. Freedom or contingency, and determination or necessity, have nothing to do with the dependence of creatures on God. They refer to the dependence of one creature on another. Or, as Aquinas puts it:

> God knows everything that happens in time with certainty and without doubt, and yet the things that happen in time are not things that must exist or must come to exist, but things that might or might not be – God's will is to be thought of as existing outside the realm of existents, as a cause from which pours forth everything that exists in all its variant forms. Now *what can be* and *what must be* are variants of being, so that it is from God's will that things derive whether or not they must be or may or may not be and the distinction of the two according to the nature of their immediate causes. For he prepares causes that must cause for those effects that he wills must be, and causes that might cause but might fail to cause for those effects that he wills might or might not be. And it is because of the nature of their causes that some effects are said to be effects that must be and others effects that need not be, although all depend on God's will as primary cause, a cause which transcends the distinction between *must* and *might not*.[9]

It was a debased form of later scholasticism which described God as *the* 'necessary being' and equated contingency with creaturehood. However, that is another story.

[9]Thomas Aquinas, *Commentary on Aristotle's 'Peri Hermeneias'*, 1 Lect. 14. I quote from Timothy McDermott (ed.), *Aquinas: Selected Philosophical Writings* (Oxford and New York: Oxford University Press, 1993), pp. 282–3.

IV The problem of evil

Now if this solution has any plausibility to you at all, you will observe that it results in a peculiarly craggy formulation of the problem of evil. It is my belief that only if we go to the limit and present it in its starkest terms do we see how it is solved. If God were less than omnipotent, if he were merely a very powerful creature, able to do some things but not others, he would manifestly be the wickedest of all creatures. However, that is to anticipate. At first sight it looks as though the Free-will Defence is some use to God. If we could say that when people act they are independent of God we could shift the blame, at least for the wickedness of the world, onto ourselves and leave God guiltless. But I have maintained that human acts, free and unfree, are done by God, so there is no get-out here for me.

We have a world completely under the control of an omnipotent God. It is a world in which there is much suffering and pain, and a world in which there is much deliberate cruelty and wickedness. Moreover, our world is one in which people who are deliberately cruel and wicked are punished and suffer for sins which God could have prevented them from committing (remember that on my view God could make everybody do good all the time without in the least interfering with their freedom). We have this world and we are expected to call this God good.

Before embarking on my answer to this difficulty, let us just notice how little you achieve by simply denying the existence of God or by denying his omnipotence. If you deny his existence, admittedly you no longer have to say things like 'God is good', but you are still left with the mystery of evil – how come the world is such a horrible place? You will have slightly less suffering if you don't believe that sinners are punished, but there will be plenty left to bother you. If you think that God exists but is not omnipotent, then, it seems to me, you have gratuitously added to the problem by inventing this vastly powerful and obviously wicked creature called God alongside all the other unpleasant things in the world. In fact all you will have achieved by eliminating God is the elimination of one logical puzzle: your sense of awe, or even resentment, at the evil in the world will remain unaffected. I mention this because all I am going to do is solve the logical puzzle, and this may seem a trivial achievement. All I am going to show is that the evil in the world is not in fact incompatible with God's goodness; I am not going to be able to show how it flows from God's goodness. When I was very small I thought that God's goodness meant that he was nice to me, and comforting and cosy in the way that my parents were. As I grew up I shed this infantile idea. I had more adult notions of what goodness can mean. But we only begin to understand God when we realize that his goodness cannot be construed on the model of any experience of our own that we have this side of heaven. Just as the child finds it difficult to understand that his parents are not being wicked when they are trying to help him, so we find it difficult to understand that God is not being wicked. But confronted with evil, this (that God is not being wicked) is the most we can hope to understand until we come to full super-human maturity in heaven.

V The nature of evil

Its reality

Let us begin by considering what we mean by evil. And first of all let us be clear that the problem of evil does not arise for someone who does not believe that evil is real. If you think that judgements of good and bad are all a matter of taste, or that it all depends on how you look at it, then the answer to the problem of evil could simply be that from where God looks at it everything is fine and dandy, and God has a taste for a little suffering here and there. You think that makes him bad? Well, that's just your taste in the matter.

No, the problem of evil only arises for people who think there is good beer and bad beer, diseased animals and healthy animals, good deeds and wicked deeds. A diseased animal is not just an animal that looks unusual to me, but an animal which has got something wrong with it in itself: an animal that is not the way animals ought to be. I do not say that all our judgements of good and bad are objective in this way. Some people would say that the alleged difference between good and bad beer is merely a matter of taste, a matter of what you are used to (I would not agree about beer, but this is obviously true of, say, fashions), but the point is that no problem of evil can arise over such subjective judgements.

Bidding goodbye, therefore, to people who do not hold that there are objective standards of good and bad, we pass on to take a closer look at what we mean by being bad.

Evil suffered and evil done

I should like first to make a broad division between evil suffered and evil done. Evil suffered is what comes to a thing from outside when it is damaged or diseased or knocked around in one way or another. Evil done is peculiar to responsible beings, it means wickedness.

Evil suffered is sometimes carelessly equated with pain, but this will not do. Pain very frequently accompanies evil suffered in the higher animals, but things which do not suffer pain, such as trees, and, I am told, beetles, can also be damaged and killed. Evil suffered just means any evil that happens to a thing for which it is not itself responsible.

If the Free-will Defence were valid, evil suffered would present the *only* problem of evil, for God, having no control over our free acts, would be unable to prevent evil done. But as we have seen, the Free-will Defence is worthless; God could always prevent any wickedness.

In fact, on my view, evil done presents a much thornier problem than evil suffered. I think a strong case could be made out for the proposition that God could not have created a material world which did not involve evil suffered. I think he could certainly have created a world without evil suffered, but not a natural material world.

Evil suffered and the perishable world

If it can be shown that evil suffered has a necessary function in the material world, then clearly it is not incompatible with the goodness of God – unless, like the Manichees, you think that matter *as such* is evil, and this would be very difficult to show. It seems to me that if we are to have a material world in which things have a certain lifetime, and grow and develop and decay and are interdependent, in particular if we are to have a world which develops in time by evolution, there is bound to be evil suffered. Pain and suffering and death have a biological function of their own, whatever other ends they may accidentally serve. It would of course have been possible for God to have made a world of animals in which, by a succession of miracles, nothing ever in fact got hurt, in which death was miraculously instantaneous and painless, and yet a world in which, miraculously, the right animals died off and the right ones survived so that the species could evolve. You have, let us say, a lion. Well, it will hardly count as a lion unless it eats lambs or some other kind of meat. So we have it eating this lamb. But, by a miracle, the lamb is anaesthetized or even enjoys being eaten. But then we need a second miracle to make the lamb run away when the lion approaches – otherwise there would be no lambs left – and so on. There would have to be an indefinite series of miracles. Such a world would, I think, be logically possible and therefore an omnipotent God could have made it. But it would not be a 'natural' world. It would be run by a series of miraculous interventions. One thing would not follow naturally from another. There would be no 'natural' order, no scientific laws. God, as I say, could have done this, but in fact he has not done so. He has made a material world which, apart from the occasional interventions we call miracles, runs itself. Things behave in a predictable way. There is a natural order in events. One of the prices for such a natural world is suffering, a price exacted not by God but by the way things are in a material world.

It might be thought, though, that there is *too much* suffering in the world, more than is strictly necessary. I think this is true in the sense that much of it is caused by the wickedness of people. Auschwitz served no biological purpose whatever. But apart from this suffering, our question can only be answered by biologists. Is there more suffering or death amongst animals than they expect? Do they sometimes say, when they come across suffering or death amongst animals, 'This is something that biology will never explain'? Mostly, I think, you will find that they explain it, or expect to explain it, without invoking a malevolent God.

Whether or not it is plausible to say that pain, and evil suffered in general, have a sufficient biological function without which we could not have real animals at all, the difficult problems arise not with evil suffered but with evil done. If we can reconcile human wickedness with the goodness of God, then the explanation will certainly cover pain as well. If it is true, as I have maintained, that my free acts are due to God, what about my sins? If God has planned and arranged everything, then it is unfair to make me sin and then send me to hell. I am now going to offer the following propositions: first, although God acts in all my activity, free and unfree, he does not make me sin; secondly, he does not send me to hell, although he does send people to heaven; thirdly, he could prevent me from sinning, and hence prevent me from going to hell, but does not always do so, yet this does not make him guilty.

ON EVIL AND OMNIPOTENCE

The relativity of evil

In order to establish these propositions I must first say a word about evil. In the first place evil suffered is relative. I mean by this that evil is always the evil of something. What is bad for one thing may be good for another. It is bad for the lamb to be eaten by the lion, but the very same action is good for the lion. I do not mean by this that evil is subjective (in the modern sense of that word). It is not just from the point of view of the lamb that what happens is bad for it. From anybody's point of view what happens is bad for the lamb, and this is not just because the lamb dislikes it (perhaps it is a masochistic lamb and enjoys it), but because eventually it dies. I should maintain that any evil suffered by one thing is always a good achieved by something else. The meal which is bad for the lamb is always good for the lion; the disease which is bad for me is a fulfilment and achievement for the germs that are causing it. It is the whole meaning of evil suffered that you are suffering from the activities and *fulfilment* of some alien being. This is why evil suffered can have a biological function. There are always two sides to it: the sufferer and the inflicter. So, there is always some thing which will get good out of it. Evil done, however, is evil that I inflict precisely on myself. The inflicter, the one who ought to be getting good out of it, is precisely the one who suffers the evil. So evil done is a dead loss. Nobody gets anything out of it, except accidentally.

Evil suffered as failure

In the second place, evil is a defect or a failure of something. This is a platitude, but it is frequently taken to be a piece of new and startling information and is hence misunderstood. What makes us assert that a dog, say, is in a bad state of health is just that it is not behaving as we think a dog should behave.

This does not necessarily mean that the dog is inactive; it may manifest its disease by hysterical leaping around and doing all kinds of energetic things, or it may manifest its illness by listlessly drooping around and doing nothing. But in both cases what makes us say that something is wrong is the failure of the beast to act as a dog ought. When we say, for example, that the television screen has a bad picture, we mean that it fails to measure up to our ideal for a television image. This may be be-. cause it is too bright or too dark, but in either case what makes us say that it is bad is its failure to be the way a television screen should be.

When we say that evil, badness, is a negation, a failure, a defect, we are sometimes thought to mean that all dogs in a bad way are inactive, or that all bad television screens are as they are due to lack of light. But this is not what we mean at all. We do not mean that all sins are sins of omission and none of commission. We mean that what precisely makes us say that something is bad (whether it is something involving a lot of activity or something involving too little activity) is its failure to be what it should be.

If an animal, human or otherwise, is sick, what is wrong is the failure of its life, whether this is due to the absence of something (as in starvation) or to the presence of something (as in cancer). When a train breaks down this may be due to too little electricity or too many rocks on the line. But it is the failure of the train to reach its destination that makes it bad.

Evil done as failure

The peculiarly moralistic education that the English suffer from can make it difficult for us to see that this is just as true of moral evil. We (some of us anyway) have been brought up to think of a certain list of activities (usually pleasant ones) as bad, wrong, unfair, not the thing, un-English, etc. And (again some of us) have been brought up to think of another list of rather tedious activities as good, decent, playing the game, praiseworthy, and so on. We acquire the impression that good and evil in moral matters are contraries – like left and right, or north and south. The thing that is wrong with this impression is this. We could alter the conventions and redraw all our maps with north at the bottom and south at the top, and we could alter our language so that left and right were interchanged, and none of this would make any difference. The maps would be as good as ever. The language would be just as intelligible. Now we can guilelessly be led into thinking that good and evil could be interchanged in the same way. We imagine someone (perhaps God) decreeing that from now on every evil will be good and every good evil. What is wrong with this, however, is not that it would be wicked but just that it would be logically impossible. Good and evil are logically related not like north and south but like north and not-north. Evil is not a positive alternative label to Good; it just means the absence of the Good label. You can't be given an instruction to redraw your maps with not-north at the top because you don't know whether this means puting south at the top or east or north-west; all these are equally not-north.

The English education inclines us not to ask why something is wrong. We just all know that this or that action is one of the wrong ones. But once we ask not just what features in the action make it wrong, but why we call it wrong or bad, what precisely its badness consists in, we find once more that it consists in a failure to be properly human, an absence of humanity in our behaviour.

When we have laboured to show that evil is a negation, an absence, a failure, there are certain to be some people who will instantly say: 'I see, you mean that evil isn't real.' But we (or I anyway) do not mean this at all. If I have a hole in my sock, the badness of this consists in the absence of wool where there ought to be some. This does not mean that the badness is illusory or unreal. If I jump out of a plane and discover that I have not got a parachute, it is of no comfort at all to be told that the absence of the parachute is not a real thing at all. When we say, 'That man has not got a beard', we cannot ask, 'Which beard has he not got?', for there is no such thing as the beard he has not got, and yet his beardlessness is a perfectly real condition.

God's activity and evil

Now in order to see what can be said about evil and the action of God let us return to the comparison I made between the presence of God and his activity. We saw that wherever anything is, we can say that God is, and similarly we can say that whenever anything acts, God acts.

Suppose that I have a tree growing in my garden. It is a good, healthy tree. We can say that God is in it keeping it in being. God is where the trunk is; he is where the branches and roots are. Now suppose that some malevolent person takes an axe and hacks away at my beautiful tree, cutting the branches off and spoiling it altogether. A passer-by will immediately notice the absence of the branches because it spoils the appearance of the tree. He will not merely notice that here we have no branches, for this is, in itself, not noticeable – after all, there are no branches in his briefcase or on his bicycle. What he notices is the absence of branches on the tree – where it makes a real difference. The absence of branches, though nothing in itself, is an evil which makes a difference to the tree, though it would not be an evil in, say, a fountain-pen. Thus, if I say, 'I have a tree in my garden', and then add, 'It has no branches', the second statement adds something to the first; whereas if I say, 'I have a fountain pen in my pocket', and then add, 'It has no branches', the second remark adds nothing that we don't already know from the first.

Now let us see where God is in the spoiled tree. We can say that God is where the trunk is and God is where the roots are, but we cannot say that God is where the branches are – for they are not there any more. We can say that God is where the air is that has replaced the branches. We can say that he is where the branches used to be. But one thing we certainly cannot say is that God is where the absence of branches is. This is no limitation on the ubiquity of God. He is not where the absence of branches is because the absence of branches isn't anywhere. And yet it is precisely this absence of branches that makes a difference to the tree and spoils it. In other words, although it is the negation, the deprivation (the absence or failure) that makes a real difference and makes us call something evil, God is not in the negation itself.

What we say of God's presence we can also say of his activity. When the locomotive is running down the track we can say that God is acting in and causing the activity of the locomotive. But when the locomotive fails we cannot say that God is acting in the failure of the machine, because the failure of the machine is not an action at all. Because we have names for failures and deprivations, and because they really happen, we are tempted to think of them as a kind of negative activity when really they are nothing at all. Because when Peter runs to kick the ball he is doing something, we are inclined to assume that when he fails to kick the ball he is doing something, a kind of shadow doing in the un-world.

Now my sins may involve a great deal of activity, but it is never the activity that makes us call them sins. What makes them sins is that this activity amounts to a failure in human living. If we abstract from my humanity and regard me for a moment as a physical object, many of my misdeeds are very energetic and active. But we do not call them bad because of this activity. We call them bad because, considered as the be-haviour of a whole human being, they represent a failure to behave in the way that human beings ought to behave.

87

Now we can certainly say that God is acting in all the activity that is involved in sinning, but he is equally certainly not acting in the failure which constitutes the sin itself.

God's activity and evil done

Let us notice a difference here between evil suffered and evil done. In all evil suffered, as we saw, there are two sides: one thing is suffering and another is acting and achieving something. For this reason we can say that God is acting in the situation of evil suffered because he is acting in the perfecting and achievement of the thing that is inflicting the suffering. God is not acting in my wasting away from disease, precisely because my wasting away is not an activity but the failure of activity, but he is acting in the activities of the germs and whatnot that bring about my disease. In this sense we can attribute evil suffered to God. We cannot, however, attribute evil done to him in any sense at all. For, as we saw, in evil done there is no achievement at all. Evil done is evil I do to myself; if it were not, I could not be blamed for it – in acting wickedly I make myself imperfect and so nobody gains by it. Other agencies can inflict physical or mental defects on me, but nothing can inflict moral defects on me. If it did, they would not be moral defects but misfortunes. Someone else can make me blind or insane, but no one else can commit my sins for me. This is exactly what defines moral evil: it is self-inflicted imperfection. Needless to say (I hope), in spite of the metaphorical language we use, God is not harmed by my sins any more than he is benefited by my worship. The good or ill effect is entirely a good or ill effect on me.

So, since there is nothing that is perfected in sin, it is a dead loss. There is nothing in which God is acting. Of course, sins can have good consequences. But the sinfulness of a sin lies not in its consequences but in the failure implied in the sin itself.

Professor Flew finds it curious and arbitrary that we should lay our faults, but not our virtues, at our door instead of God's.[10] In a footnote he suspects that, for some people, the 'elusive doctrine' of the negativity of evil may remove the arbitrariness.[11] I hope it is now clear that the logical *platitude* that evil is a deprivation does begin to make a difference between our virtues and our faults. At least, so far we can say that in our good deeds, which are achievements, God is positively acting; whereas in our bad deeds, which are failures of achievement, he is not positively acting. But, adds Professor Flew, 'who is there but God who could have left the gaps?'[12] In other words, even if we cannot indict God for positively making us sin (since sin is not a positive achievement), surely we can indict him for neglect in not making us achieve our perfection. What difference does it make, after all, whether I murder someone by hitting them with a hammer or by failing to apply the brake of my car? It would make a difference, of course, if I were *unable* to apply the brake. But nobody but the Free-will Defence people thinks that God is unable to make me virtuous. Is God then guilty of the evil in the world by neglect? If he is, then he is surely just as wicked as if evil were a positive creature which he had created. The English mind especially is apt to be impatient with such legal and scholastic hairsplitting.

Is God guilty by neglect?

But what exactly does it mean to be guilty by neglect? If a doctor through laziness neglects his training and, as a consequence of his incompetence, one of his patients dies, he may be guilty by neglect. If a mother does not feed her child for a long time,

---

[10]Flew, 'Divine Omnipotence and Human Freedom', p. 167.
[11]Ibid., n. 37.
[12]Ibid.

and it dies, she may be guilty by neglect. Guilt by neglect is incurred when there is something that you are able to do and ought to do and you do not do it. It is important to emphasize the 'ought to do' here. If terrorists capture my father and announce that they will kill him unless I betray military secrets to them, or whatever, I am in a position to save my father only by doing something I am *able* to do but not something I *ought* to do. If I refuse to do this, and if the terrorists kill my father, I am clearly not guilty by neglect of his death. If we are to make out a sound case against God as guilty by neglect, we have to show not only that he is able to prevent me sinning but also that he ought to. Yet this latter suggestion is clearly untrue. A doctor *ought* to know about medicine. A mother *ought* to feed her child. For everything with a function in the world, there is something that fulfils that function, there are certain things it ought to do if we are going to call it good. If we are going to call them good, a doctor has to know his job, and a mother has to care for her child. But clearly we do not call God good because he fulfils some function.

When the steam-engine breaks down we say that the engine has failed because it is not making the wheels go round. Making the wheels go round is what the engine is for. The fact that the wheels do not go round is not a failure on the part of the engine-driver's whiskers because this is not what the whiskers are for. Similarly, not to make the wheels go round is not a failure on the part of God, because making the wheels go round is not what God is for. God is not for anything, there is nothing that he ought to do. It is only of things that have a function within the world that we can speak of what they are for. We can say, '*This* is the sort of activity we expect of a fountain-pen, as opposed to *that* sort of activity.' But we cannot say, 'This is the sort of activity we expect of God.' We say, 'That is a good fountain-pen because it behaves as a fountain-pen should.' We cannot say, 'God is good because he behaves as a God should.' God is not a divine kind of thing in the way in which a man is a human kind of thing. He has no certain defined and prescribed field of activity and perfection. When we say that God is good we do not mean he is well-behaved.

When, therefore, I act in a less than human way, this is a failure on my part because acting in a human way is what *I* am for. But the fact that God has not made me act in a human way is not a failure on his part because this is not what *he* is for. It needs a kind of cosmic megalomania to suppose that God has the job of saving my soul and is to be given bad marks if he does not do that. Whatever he does for us, like creating us in the first place, is an act of gratuitous love, not something that is demanded of him.

What does 'God is good' mean?

There is, however, one final difficulty in all this. If when we say that God is good we do not mean that he is well-behaved, what do we mean? To put it another way, if we are going to call God good whatever unimaginable horrors may turn up in his world, if we are just going to keep on chanting 'God is good' with the same degree of conviction, whatever evidence may be presented to us in the world, does not the phrase seem to be 'freewheeling' – just going round without doing any work?

Well, let us see where we have got to. What do we know of God? We know that everything he does is good, for there is no good achievement of anything, whether in nature or in man, which is not done by God. It is true that these are not achievements *of* God, but the achievements of other things that he brings about. Nevertheless, they are good, and they are his work. We also know that God does nothing that is evil. He does some good things which result in evils suffered (his doing good for the lion is bad for the lamb). As I have argued, however, if you think it good to have a material, natural, perishable world, this seems inevitable. Always to do what is good and never to do what is evil – is this not a sufficient reason for being called good? Certainly God could do more good than he has done. He could have created yet more creatures, yet more worlds; he could have saved even more souls. He could even have made everybody virtuous, but unless you hold the ridiculous view that it is his *job* to make the maximum number of perfect creatures, clearly the fact that he has not done everything does not detract from his goodness. Every positive thing in the world, every evidence of vitality, every virtue, is evidence for the goodness of God and justification for saying that he is good. It is true that not everything we see is evidence for the goodness of God (sin is not evidence for the goodness of God), but the point is that it is not evidence for his badness. This odd situation arises because we do not see the goodness of God in itself. The meaning we give to phrases like 'the goodness of God', or the word 'God' itself, derives *not* from what we know of the nature of God but from what we know of *creatures*. It is as though we only had a few fragments of a map of God. Everything we can see on the map points to his goodness, but there are many bits missing. The holes in the map (sin and evil) are places where God is not shown to be good. They are not places where he is shown not to be good. The world is a bad map of God. But it is not a map of a bad God.

Since, as philosophers, we only know of God from the world he has made, we cannot answer the question why he made this world rather than another. This is not to deny that there is 'reason besides his will', but merely to confess our ignorance of it. And of course this has nothing in common with the idea that morality has no foundation except the arbitrary will of God. Moral notions, I should say, are notions about the goodness and badness of human acts as such, and are defined by the nature of human beings. Certainly, when I do right I do what God wills, but God's will for me is shown in his giving me this human nature. God invented morality automatically when he invented human beings – just as he invented entomology automatically when he invented beetles.

What I have been trying to do in this essay, albeit briefly, is to solve the puzzle about omnipotence, freedom and evil. All I have given you is a rather inelegant restatement of a very traditional solution. I hope, nevertheless, that it has disentangled the puzzle. But when it is finished we must admit that we have not got very far. We are no clearer than when we started about why there should be wickedness in the world. It is one thing to know that the proposition that some creatures are evil is not incompatible with the proposition that the Creator is omnipotent and good. It would be quite another thing to understand the mysterious goodness of the Creator. When all is said and done, we are left with an irrational but strong feeling that if we were God we would have acted differently. Perhaps one of his reasons for acting as he did is to warn us not to try to make him in our own image.

7

A Very Short Introduction to Aquinas

I

A friend of mine claims that once in a restaurant he overheard one waiter saying to another waiter: 'He's eaten it.' When you catch a snippet of conversation like that you begin to be puzzled about its context. It's going to be a little like that with what follows. We are going to overhear fragments of talk, and I am going to try to fit them into a context.

Imagine you are passing the open window of a lecture room in the University of Paris one autumn in the thirteenth century. The room is crowded with young men who are going to be teachers or preachers (or both), and their lecturer, a Dominican friar called Thomas Aquinas, is starting his course of lectures by telling them that if they are going to teach or preach they themselves must first of all be taught by God:

> God has destined us for a goal beyond the grasp of reason – *No eye has seen what you have prepared for those who love you* – and since we must set ourselves this goal and pursue it we needed teaching about it beforehand. We even need revealed instruction in things reason can learn about God. If such truths had been left to us to discover, they would have been learnt by few over long periods and mingled with much error; yet our whole well-being is centred on God and depends on knowing them. So, in order

that more of us might more safely attain him, we need teaching in which God revealed himself.[1]

Aquinas treats theology as a practical matter. He is not interested in spinning theories about angels and the points of a pin. He is concerned with human well-being. Behind what he says is the image of people going somewhere: we have a 'goal', and (more mysteriously) a goal 'beyond the grasp of reason'. Human well-being, he thinks, is a kind of journey, but a journey into the unknown, towards a destination we only dimly perceive by faith. I think here of the medieval folktale of the youngest son going out to seek his fortune. I used to think that he was going out in search of a fortune, a whole lot of money, but of course he wasn't: he went to seek his *fortuna*, his luck.

For Aquinas the goal is already partly with us in the journey itself. For him the world is good – but not good enough. For him there is no evil in this material creation. Everything that is, is good. Every being has God within it holding it in being. It is just that some goods are greater than others. Evil comes in when we neglect some great good for the sake of some trivial good: when we sacrifice, say, being just and loving for the sake of being rich. Evil, for Aquinas, is a purely spiritual thing. It belongs to the world of minds and policies and decisions – and even there it is not a positive thing but a failure, a failure to want the good enough. The material world, however, is innocent, and more than innocent; it is the scintillating manifestation of the love of God.

All the more important, then, that we get our priorities right, and, to a certain extent, we can get them right if we keep our

---

[1]Thomas Aquinas, *Summa Theologiae*, Ia, 1, 1; the biblical quotation is from 1 Cor. 2.9. All translations of Aquinas in this essay come from Timothy McDermott (ed.), *St Thomas Aquinas, 'Summa Theologiae': A Concise Translation* (London: Eyre Spottiswoode, 1989). For the present passage see p. 1.

emotions in order and exercise ordinary good sense. We can try to use maps, but, in the end, ours is a journey without maps because it is a journey beyond the human horizon, a journey towards living with God himself. We are fortunate enough, lucky enough, to be personal friends of God – this good luck is what Thomas calls 'grace'. So our journey is really more like a treasure-hunt – we are guided only by certain clues. But God, Aquinas is telling his students, is generous even with the clues. He tells us not only things we couldn't know of ourselves. He even tells us some things that we might have found out for ourselves if we were clever enough. And he does this, says Aquinas, because the journey to human well-being is not just for intellectuals, not just for an elite, the well-educated, the perceptive. God has distributed his clues to all of us, showing us how our lives can be more human, showing us how we can become divine, because he loves all of us.

II

Thomas Aquinas thought that theologians don't know what they are talking about. They try to talk about God, but Aquinas was most insistent that they do not, and cannot know what God is. He was, I suppose, the most agnostic theologian in the Western Christian tradition – not agnostic in the sense of doubting whether God exists, but agnostic in the sense of being quite clear and certain that God is a *mystery* beyond any understanding we can now have.

He was sure that God *is* because he thought that there must *be* an answer to the deepest and most vertiginous question, 'Why is there anything instead of nothing at all?' But he was also sure that we do not know what that answer is. To say it is God who made the whole universe, and holds it continually in existence from moment to moment (as singers hold their songs in existence from moment to moment), is not to *explain* how the universe comes to exist. For we do not know what we mean by 'God'. We use this word just as a convenient label for something we do not understand. For Aquinas, only God understands what God is. Aquinas thought that in the Bible God has promised us that one day he will give us a share in his self-understanding, but not yet. Until that day, although God has begun to reveal himself in his Word made flesh, we grasp his self-communication not by coming to know, but only by faith. Faith is an illumination that appears as darkness: we come to know that we do not know.

Aquinas thought we know of God only by trying to understand the things he has done and does for us – the marvellous works of his creation, the even more marvellous works of his salvation, God's personal love for creatures who have rejected him by sin – the whole story that he tells us in the Bible. But none of these works are adequate to show us God himself – no more than you could come to understand the mind of Shakespeare or Beethoven by hearing them ask you to pass the salt:

> Our natural knowledge starts from sense-perception and reaches only as far as things so perceived can lead us, which is not far enough to see God in himself. For the things we sense, though effects of God, are not effects fully expressing his power. But because they do depend on him as their cause, they can lead us to know that he exists, and reveal to us whatever is true of him as first cause of all such things, surpassingly different from all of them ... God's gracious revelation ... strengthens our natural light of intelligence ... Although in this life revelation cannot show us what God is in himself, but joins us to him as unknown, nevertheless it helps us to know him better, showing us more and greater works of his.[2]

---

[2] *Summa Theologiae*, Ia, 12, 12 and 12, 13 (McDermott, *St Thomas Aquinas*, p. 29).

For Thomas Aquinas, our proper and reasonable response to God is not one of exact analysis but of prayer. People who think they have no belief quite often say that they want to pray but do not know who or what they could be praying to. Aquinas would *not* say to such people, 'Ah, but you see, if you became a believer, a Christian, we would change all that. You would come to understand to whom you are praying.' Not at all. He would say to such people, 'If you became a Christian you would stop being surprised by or ashamed of your condition. You would be happy with it. For faith would assure you that you *could not* know what God is until he reveals himself to us openly.' Praying without knowing, or expecting to know, to whom you are praying is the normal and natural way for a Christian. For now what matters is not knowledge; what matters is faith and confidence in the love of God for us, and the courage to share in that love and pass it on to others – until the time when God's promise is fulfilled. 'For now we see in a mirror, dimly, but then we will see face to face. Now I know only in part; then I will know fully, even as I have been fully known' (1 Cor. 13.12).

III

According to Thomas Aquinas, if God is the cause of *all* that is, we can at least be sure that nothing can be the cause of God. This, says Aquinas, makes a radical difference between the way we love and the way God loves. For our love is caused by the goodness and attractiveness of what we love, but this cannot be the case with God. He does not love things or people because they are good; on the contrary, they are good and attractive because God loves them. God's love is creative; it brings about the goodness of what he loves. When, as it says in the beginning of the book of Genesis, 'God saw everything that he had made, and indeed, it was very good' (Gen. 1.31), God was not discovering its goodness. He was not struck with admiration by its beauty. Its goodness and beauty were his doing, the work of his love. For Aquinas, the entire universe, from each single raindrop to the furthest galaxies, exists because at every moment it is known and loved by God. The reason why God cannot love sin and evil is simply that 'sin' and 'evil' are not the names of things. They are defects, failures, nonbeing in otherwise good things. If I am sinful it is because I am failing to live up to what my humanity demands of me. I am failing to be just, kind, gentle or loving. I am failing to have that intense, passionate love for God's creation and God himself that would make me a fully developed human being. So God does not make sin and evil any more than he makes the elephant that is not in my garden. He makes all that does exist, and makes it by love:

> Everything that exists is, as such, good, and has God as its cause. Clearly then God loves all things, willing them every good they possess; yet not as we do. Our love doesn't cause a thing's goodness; rather the thing's goodness, real or imagined, evokes our love, and enlists our help in preserving and furthering that goodness. But God's love evokes and creates the goodness in things ... God loves sinners as beings he has created, but he hates their sinning, which is a way of not being and is not God's doing. God loves everything with the same simple uniform act of will; but just as we love those persons more to whom we will greater good, even when we will it with no greater intensity, so too with God. God causes the goodness in things, and one thing would not be better than another unless God loved it more.[3]

So God's love is at the centre of every existing thing, the deepest reality in every existing thing. The special point about human beings, however, which is not shared by other animals,

---

[3]Ibid., Ia, 20, 2 (cf. McDermott, *St Thomas Aquinas*, pp. 156f.).

is that we can lay hold on ourselves, on the centre of our being, by knowledge and love. Of course, other animals can know and love too, but not in the very profound sense in which we are able to do so by our capacity for symbolizing and articulating our world in language. Because we have this capacity to understand and to love, God can give us the capacity to respond to his love at the centre of our being. God strengthens our understanding by the gift of faith and strengthens our loving by the gift of charity, so that we share in *his* self-understanding and in *his* loving. It is true that our share in God's self-understanding does not yet make God clear to us – that is something we are promised for the future. For the present, faith is more like a darkness. But we walk confidently in this dark, for we have learned not to put our trust in the specious and beguiling lights which fall short of the truth of God.

Faith is only the beginning of our sharing in God's self-knowledge, in God's Word, and, as St Paul tells us, it will pass away as it is transformed into the vision of God (1 Cor. 13.8–12). But our sharing in God's loving, in that creative love in which he makes all things, our *charity*, will not pass away. The power to love as God loves, the power to share in his creativity, is the life we shall share for eternity.

IV

Thomas Aquinas thought that God created a world with its own order, with its own natural causes within it. So we can explain the characteristic behaviour of one sort of thing by referring to the behaviour of another kind of thing within creation. Magnetic needles point to the north because of the earth's magnetic field, and in its turn, a magnetic field is caused by the behaviour of subatomic particles.

These are not, of course, Aquinas's own examples, but, like most of us, he thought that there were causes in this world, and causes of these causes – a sort of hierarchical order of causes (like a chain of command). And this whole explanatory order, he thought, was created and sustained in being by God. He also thought it was the business of the natural sciences to trace this order of natural explanations (to show how the universe explains its own character). For this reason, he thought that there was no need for scientists to bring God into their scientific explanations. God is simply presupposed to be at the heart of the existence of the whole world that the scientist studies. It is quite true that God causes the kettle to boil, as he causes everything, but the scientist is interested in the natural created causes that God uses to bring about this effect. Physicists may well be driven to ask, 'What is the explanation of there being anything at all instead of nothing at all?', but if they ask this, they are no longer doing physics. Aquinas would have been surprised and amused by the idea that in studying what seems to have happened in the first moments of the Big Bang we are somehow studying the act of creation. The creative act of God is not, for him, something *unique* to the beginning (if there was, indeed, a beginning), but to the continuing existence of anything at any time. In fact, he thought that God could easily have created a world which never had a beginning. For him the creative act of God is at work within the working of every creature all the time.

What, then, does he think about miracles? He says that God's activity is deep within everything and that nature's activities are to be attributed to God working within nature. But Aquinas also thinks that God, if he wants to, can override created causes so that he himself produces their normal effects or effects beyond their power.[4] So Aquinas didn't see miracles as God intervening to interfere with the world. God, thinks Aquinas, cannot literally intervene in the universe because he is always there – just as much in the normal, natural run of things as in the

4Cf. ibid., Ia, 105, 6.

resurrection of Christ or in any other miraculous event. A miracle, for Aquinas, is not a special *presence* of God; it is a special absence of natural causes – a special absence that makes the perpetual presence of God more visible to us. Since God is there all the time, and since he doesn't need to be mentioned when we are doing physics or biology, or doing the shopping, we may be in danger of forgetting him. So a miracle, in Aquinas's view, is an exuberant gesture, like an embrace or a kiss, to say, 'Look, I'm here; I love you', lest in our wonder and delight at the works of his creation we forget that all that we have and all we are is the radiance of his love for us.

V

What is it to be a good person? What is it to live well rather than badly? We might say, 'It is to act in accordance with some true moral code.' If we are Christians or Jews, we might mention the moral code of the ten commandments. If we say this, however, we will find at least one person who disagrees with us, and that is Thomas Aquinas. He did not think that living well consists in acting in accordance with the commandments. This is not because he thought (as some modern Christians do) that the commandments have been superseded by the law of love. He thought the ten commandments were just a common-sense account of what loving behaviour is like (and especially what it is *not* like). He thought that any society which was indifferent to whether you broke the commandments or not couldn't be a community of friends. He thought these commandments were one of those things given to us by God in his revelation which we could have worked out for ourselves, if we thought hard and honestly enough about what a society based on friendship would be like.

But although Aquinas holds the moral code of the commandments in high esteem, he would still disagree with you if you said that living well is simply acting in accordance with the commandments. Why? Because, he says, living well is not *just* a matter of doing good things instead of bad things. It is a matter of doing them *well*, and that means doing them from the depths of your real character.

You may do an act of kindness, you may send a donation for the relief of famine, say, in Africa, because you have been momentarily swayed by television reporting or whatever, and that, of course, is a good thing to do. You may do it because you have been told that it is the right thing for a Christian to do. You may do it because you fear that God will punish you if you don't, and it is still a good thing to do. But Aquinas would say that this is still not what living well means. Living well means doing good because you *want* to do it, because you have become the kind of *you* that just naturally wants to do this. Then you are no longer just doing kind *acts*. You are a kind *person*:

Living well is not only doing good things, but doing them well, choosing them in a right way and not simply acting on impulse or emotion. Right choosing involves having a right goal and suitably acting to achieve that goal. The dispositions to right goals are the moral virtues in the appetites; the disposition to act suitably to achieve the goal must dispose reason to plan and decide well, and that is the virtue of prudence. Doing something good on another's advice rather than one's own judgment is not yet a perfect activity of one's own reasoning and desiring. One does the good but not altogether well, as living requires. Thinking in a theoretical way seeks the true match of mind to things ... Thinking practically seeks the true match to right appetite, and that can only happen in ... matters we have power to influence ... So the virtues concerned with contingent matters are dispositions of practical thought: skill for making, prudence for doing. In the case of doing, man's practical reasoning makes plans and decisions just as his theoretical reasoning explores and arrives at conclusions, but then goes on to issue commands to do things, and that is its special role. If men made good decisions and then didn't implement them properly, reason's work would be incomplete.[5]

So Aquinas thought we become good, we live well, by acquiring a *character*, a complex set of dispositions which incline us, first of all, to want good things (and to want greater goods more than lesser goods), and then to think well in a practical way (to be wise) about how to achieve these goods. These dispositions are *virtues*, and we acquire them normally by *practice*. First, we do good things because we want to please our parents or others, or because we want to follow some moral code. But, gradually, such behaviour becomes second nature to us, and then, and *only* then, do we have the virtues. Then we are grown-up. Then when we do good actions they are our *own*, springing from the personality we have created for ourselves with the help of others. That's what education is, or ought to be.

But, of course, Aquinas thought that we are not simply called by God to live well as human beings, but to live the life of God; and this is the sheer gift of God. So God, besides giving us clues to guide us on our way to him, also gives us the power to make the journey. He begins to share his own life with us and so gives us the virtues we need to live well both humanly and divinely – and gives them as a free grace, bypassing the laborious educational process.

VI

That great English Tory Dr Johnson declared, 'I have always said the first Whig was the Devil.' That great English Whig (or

[5]Ibid., IaIIae, 57, 5–6 (McDermott, *St Thomas Aquinas*, p. 236, with slight alterations).

Liberal) Lord Acton said, 'The first Whig was not the Devil, but Thomas Aquinas.' I am not sure that Aquinas would have been altogether pleased with that compliment. Certainly he had no time for Liberal free-market economics and unrestrained competition. He thought that it was the business of the state to care for all the people, especially the poor, and in some cases to intervene to decree maximum prices and minimum wages. He thought that the purpose of law was not just to protect people from each other, but to help them all to be virtuous and, therefore, most likely to be happy in this world. He would undoubtedly have welcomed the welfare state.

He would have disagreed strongly with Margaret Thatcher when she said, 'There is no such thing as society, only individuals and their families.' He was more subtle than that. He said that the individual is essentially a part of society, and that the good of the whole society is greater than the good of the individual. But he also thought that the whole society exists for the sake of the good lives of its individuals.

Aquinas was a Whig or Liberal in that he had no time for any notion of the 'divine right of kings', or the divine right of the party, and would rejoice at the collapse of dictatorships. He said that the authority of rulers and their laws comes only from the consent of the governed, and he said that 'planning for the general good belongs to the people as a whole, or to those who represent them'.[6] He thought that a legitimate representative of the people, ruling with their consent and making laws for the common good (and not just for the good of this or that class or section within society), was ruling justly. In so far as he or she ruled justly, he or she ruled with the authority of God, but *only* in so far as he or she ruled justly:

Humanly enacted laws can be just or unjust. To be just they must serve the general good, must not exceed the

[6]Ibid., IaIIae, 96, 4 (McDermott, *St Thomas Aquinas*, p. 291).

lawmaker's authority, and must fairly apportion the burdens of the general good amongst all members of the community. Such just laws oblige us in conscience since they derive from the eternal law. Laws however can be unjust: by serving not the general good but some lawmaker's own greed or vanity, or by exceeding his authority, or by unfairly apportioning the burdens the general good imposes. Such laws are not so much laws as forms of violence, and do not oblige our consciences except perhaps to avoid scandal and disorder, on which account men must sometimes forego their right. Laws can also be unjust by running counter to God's good, promoting idolatry say; and nobody is allowed to obey such laws: *we must obey God rather than men.*[7]

Aquinas thought that an unjust society which discriminates against some section of the people on grounds of racism or ideology or religious bigotry, or any other grounds, is already a society of violence rather than law – long before any dissidents seek to overthrow it. Law, says Aquinas, is only just, and only genuine law, if it is an expression of morality. On the other hand, however, Aquinas did not think it the business of law to repress every immorality, for, he believed, this may often do more damage to the common good than tolerating a wicked practice. Here, said Aquinas, rulers must use their common sense, their wisdom, to decide whether or not some particular human behaviour should be a crime. Aquinas, for instance, thought that abortion was sinful and a great human evil. But, when you have said that, you have not yet decided whether and how it should be forbidden by law. That is something Aquinas would think open to discussion amongst people all equally committed to the sanctity of all human life. Yes, perhaps he was the first Whig.

[7] Ibid. The biblical quotation is from Acts 5.29.

VII

It would be quite generally agreed that the foundation of Christian morality is that people should love each other. Thomas Aquinas, interestingly, did not agree. Of course, it depends on what you mean by 'love'. You can love your mother, good wine, your country and your boyfriend – each with a different kind of love. When it comes to love in its most fundamental sense, however, Aquinas thought that the author of the first letter of John had got it right: 'In this is love, not that we loved God but that he loved us and sent his Son' (1 John 4.10). Love is, first of all, what *God* has for us; indeed this love *is* God. God loves us so much that he lets us share in his own power of loving. We have a special name for our sharing in God's power to love: we call it *charity.*

This divine charity of ours, says Aquinas, is first of all our response to God's love for us. So first there is the mutual love which makes us friends with God, sharing in his life and joy. This is the foundation of Christian morality: not a code of conduct but our friendship with God, or sharing in his Spirit, which shows itself in our love for God's friends and creatures. But our friendship with God, says Aquinas, surprisingly but profoundly, does not first overflow into love of others. First of all, he insists, we must love ourselves. If we do not love ourselves, we cannot love others.

There is a kind of fake altruism in which we can busy ourselves with others because we fear that, if we really considered ourselves, we would hate what we see. But charity means that we are able to take a clear look at ourselves, warts and all, and yet love ourselves in charity as God does. This is not selfishness. Selfishness comes from loving not our whole selves but just that part of ourselves that is our bodily life and our bodily possessions (in which we can be in competition with others). In charity I am concerned for the flourishing and happiness of my whole self, including the health and strength and liveliness of my body, but not excluding even more important things like my attitudes to others:

> Strictly speaking we don't have friendship for ourselves but something more: a love of self which is at the root of all friendship, since in friendship we love others as we love ourselves. But charity is friendship first with God and secondly with all who belong to God including ourselves. So we love ourselves with charity, inasmuch as we too are God's. When we blame people for self-love it is because they love ... their bodily natures, not loving what is genuinely good for themselves as rational beings ... Our bodies were created by God, not ... by some evil principle. So we can serve God with our bodies, and should love them with the charity with which we love God. What we shouldn't love is the taint of sin and the damage it has wreaked in our bodies; we should rather long with charity for an end of all that. Our body helps us to happiness, and that happiness will overflow into our bodies, so that they too can be loved with charity.[8]

Thomas Aquinas is a very long way from those people, including some Christians, who think that the body, and especially our bodily pleasures and emotions, are to be feared and avoided. He thought that we must learn to love and take delight in our bodily life (as God does) – giving it its due place and dignity. For God loves our bodily selves not only as creatures but as personal friends. Aquinas says in one place that separation from God by sin has so distorted our emotional life that we do not enjoy sex enough.[9]

For Aquinas, it is only heretics who dislike and despise the body. For him the Word of God to us is not, first of all, words

---

[8]Ibid., IIaIIae, 25, 4 and 5 (McDermott, *St Thomas Aquinas*, p. 355, with slight alterations).
[9]Cf. Ibid., Ia, 98, 2, ad. 3.

in a book. It is the Word made flesh, through whose body and blood we are brought back to friendship with God, so that at the resurrection of the body the divine life will overflow into our bodies in eternity.

VIII

Not very many people can claim to understand just where physics is going nowadays, but sixty or so years ago we were hearing that the behaviour of things depended on their atoms, and that atoms consisted of rings of electrons spinning around a nucleus. Each atom was a bit like a tiny solar system, and the familiar visible goings-on in the world were more or less determined by the structure of these revolving systems of particles.

Remembering this may help us to understand how Aquinas, in the thirteenth century, saw the physical world. His picture was remarkably similar, except that the spinning objects that determined the laws of physics and chemistry, instead of being very much smaller than our familiar objects, were very much bigger. He inherited the ancient belief that the revolutions of the stars and the planets played much the same part as the modern spinning of subatomic particles: they accounted for the regular, predictable behaviour of physical objects. Aquinas was quite wrong, of course, but his ideas about how far the stars determine happenings on earth remain, perhaps, relevant when we ask how far the mechanisms studied by modern scientists determine what goes on.

Medieval people were almost as superstitious as modern people, and fascinated by 'what the stars foretell'. But Aquinas was very sceptical about all that. He thought that the stars could affect us physically, and so, like tranquillizers or alcohol or lack of sleep, could affect our emotions and feelings, and incline us to certain kinds of behaviour. *Incline* us, but not *determine* us, for we can stop and think, and we can deliberately cultivate patterns of reasonable behaviour (virtues), so that we won't be dominated by the feelings of the moment. In this way we can escape slavery to the stars (so Aquinas thought).

Nevertheless, because a great many people don't bother to think or to learn how to be reasonable, they are swept away by their feelings and prejudices. That, Aquinas thought, is why astrologers can often be right statistically about majority behaviour – rather like sociologists predicting (or at least explaining) trends or voting patterns:

> Clearly events which happen necessarily can be predicted with the help of the stars, in the way astronomers predict eclipses. But the stars neither signify nor cause future chance events... Nor can the stars cause free acts of reason and will; bodies cannot directly affect our mind and will, which are neither bodily nor functions of bodily organs. The stars can cause changes in human bodies, and so influence our sensual desires which are functions of bodily organs. So the stars can incline us to certain behaviour. But since... our sensual desires obey reason, man still has a free will to act against the influence of the stars. So, trying to predict chance events or human behaviour from an inspection of the stars is pointless... This doesn't preclude prediction of things which are truly effects of the stars, like drought and rainfall and suchlike. Moreover, the stars cause changes in our bodies and influence our emotions, and since most men follow their emotions without controlling them, astrologers often get things right, especially when predicting group behaviour.[10]

For Aquinas, the constant movement of the stars, and the regular behaviour of nature governed by this, is the work of God the Creator. But the works of human intelligence are an even

---

[10]Ibid., IIaIIae, 95, 5 (McDermott, *St Thomas Aquinas*, p. 413, with slight alterations).

greater manifestation of God's power. The things we do because we decide to do so for our own reasons (and not because we are the playthings of physical causes), these *free* acts, are not brought about by any created things, but are directly created by God.

So Aquinas did not think that our freedom makes us independent of God's creative energy (nothing that exists could be that). But it makes us independent of other creatures. For Aquinas, we can stand over against all the forces of nature because of the creative work of God within us. We are free not *in spite of* God, but *because of* God. So human freedom, human creativity, is the greatest manifestation in the world of God's creative love – except for that most free of all human beings, who was himself God's love in the flesh amongst us.

8

Aquinas on 'God is Good'

When we ask ourselves whether God is good we are inclined to think along these lines: God is some kind of person, so to ask whether God is good is to ask whether he is a good person, to ask whether we can attribute to him the characteristics of good people. Is he kind and considerate and just and honest?

Aquinas, to whom I am much indebted when it comes to the topic of God's goodness, decides that some of the words we use in describing good people can be applied to God. But not for reasons as simple-minded as these. He thinks it makes sense to speak of God as just and truthful and loving, and to deny that he is unjust or untruthful. But words which designate moral virtues in human beings do not in the same sense refer to the morality of God. God is not, in this sense, morally good – not, of course, because like tigers and tables he is below the moral level, but because he transcends it. God could not be morally good, still less could he be morally bad, as he could not be physically strong or feeble, healthy or sick. Moral goodness and badness belong to beings which consciously and freely attain, or seek by rational choice to attain, their perfection – a perfection they might or might not have had. Plainly, Aquinas cannot think of God in this way. For according to him there is no potentiality in God, no unfulfilled possibility, or even fulfilled possibility. It never makes sense to say that God might not have been what he actually is. Nor of course could God be rational or irrational or make choices: these things belong to material animals which understand by the use of language or other material symbols. So what *does* Aquinas mean by saying that God is good?

He begins by asking what 'good' means. In its most general sense, he thinks, following Aristotle, that what is good is what is aimed at or sought. It is connected with appetite or tendency, or desire. As truth is what is known, goodness is what is wanted. What is good is what is wanted, to be good is to be attractive. Thus a good bicycle is a bicycle that someone would want if he wanted a bicycle and wanted it simply for being a *bicycle*. You might want a bicycle for very special purposes – for example, as a weapon, or as an object in an artistic composition. And then you might not necessarily want a good bicycle. But if you want it for what bicycles are characteristically for, for *cycling*, then other things being equal, a good one is just what you will want.

It follows, of course, that goodness is not some common property of things, like roundness or redness, but a function of the nature or role of a thing. The features that make a bicycle a good one are not the features that make an elephant or a glass of whiskey a good one. For this way of thinking, a good X is an X which has whatever features are desirable in that *kind* of thing, an X kind of thing. A bad X would be an X which lacked some such features. For Aquinas, to say that something is bad is always to indicate that it lacks some feature required for its goodness. Being bad, like being *deaf* or *absent* or *fake* or *neutral*, is always *not* being something. Aquinas thought that we become very confused about the so-called 'problem of evil' if we overlook this elementary logical point, if we imagine that badness is a positive feature of things. He does not mean that what is bad always lacks some bit or part, as though a bad X were always *smaller* than a good X. For a thing may be bad, it may lack desirable features, through having unwanted extras as well as through having bits missing. A bad washing-machine, one that fails to wash the clothes, may be so because it doesn't have enough bits (driving belts), or has too much (someone has filled it up with glue). A bad human being, one who fails in, say, the virtue of temperateness, may be so through being filled with strange passions and energies. But more of this later.

Aquinas now considers the notion of perfection. The perfect means, literally, the 'thoroughly made' (from *per* and *facere*). I could botch together something that would be recognizable, and even viable, as a bicycle, but only if I go on to make it *thoroughly*, to give it all the features desirable in a bicycle, does it begin to approach perfection. Other things being equal, if I want to make a bicycle, I will necessarily want to make a good bicycle. The good bicycle will be just what I am aiming at, even though I may not make it thoroughly enough to achieve this aim. Of course, there may be special circumstances in which what I want is precisely to make a bad bicycle (for my enemy, let us say, so that the brakes will fail at a sharp bend when going downhill). But the point is that these are always *special* circumstances. There do not have to be special circumstances for me to aim at making a good bicycle. It is sufficient that I simply want to make a good bicycle.

If you were to watch a bicycle being made, and if you understood the process, you would see the bicycle approaching perfection. To understand the process just is to see it as a making, a movement towards being thoroughly made. This process is at one and the same time the fulfilment of the aim of the bicycle-maker *as* bicycle-maker, and the fulfilment or perfecting of the bicycle itself. *The thing before us becomes a perfected and good bicycle just in so far as it attains the end set for it by its maker, which is also the aim set for herself by its maker.* It is a characteristic difference between Aristotelians (like Aquinas) and Platonists that for the Platonists the ideal or model of a thing by which we judge it (and to which it never fully attains) is a Form or pattern already existing in an immaterial world apart, laid up in heaven, so to say, while for the Aristotelian it is a form or pattern in the aim or intention of the maker. Of course, this is easy to see with human-made artefacts; it is the makers who decide what they are aiming at, and it is by their success or failure in attaining it that they judge their artefact to be good or bad.

Aquinas, however, seeks to apply the same sort of language to natural things: a horse is a good horse in that it attains the aim intended by the maker of horses. Now what does this mean?

In the first place, the maker in question can't be simply the parents of some particular horse (a defective horse is not simply a disappointment to its parents), for the parents of a horse simply produce a repetition of themselves; they are not the makers that determine what *sort of thing* a horse is – in, for example, the way that a bicycle-maker does determine what sort of thing a bicycle is, and so determines what would count as a good, successfully made bicycle. The parents' actions simply determine that there shall be another individual horse. They do not bring it about that there should be horses at all. For evidently the parents themselves are horses already, as were their grandparents and great-grandparents, indefinitely, and they could not bring it about that they themselves are horses. The maker in question, by whose aims the goodness or badness of a horse is to be assessed, must be the second-order maker who determines *what it is to be a horse* in the way that the bicycle-maker (who is not himself a bicycle) determines what it is to be a bicycle.

Suppose that I were to construct a computerized machine, and suppose I were to program it to collect together materials and to shape them into another computer of exactly the same kind, which would, of course, *eo ipso*, be programmed to make yet another. And so on. There does not seem to be anything incongruous or logically odd about this, and, indeed, it seems to be rather like what we see around us in the plants and beasts. Each of these computers could be seen as aiming at replicating another, identical computer, though, of course, this does not imply any conscious purpose or choice in them. It is simply *what they tend to do*, being the kind of things they are. This tendency itself is built into them by the manufacturer, who determined that they should be *this kind* of machine, having *this* design. Such a manufacturer could be called a *second*-order cause of each computer in the series. The *first*-order cause is the machine immediately before it in the series, which brings it about that there shall be another, identical individual machine. The second-order cause would be the manufacturer, who determined, perhaps chose, the design and programming of the computers, and thereby determined what operations they perform and what they would be (so to say) 'aiming at'. Such a computer would be a good (non-defective) one if it fulfilled this aim of the manufacturer, *qua* manufacturer, who determined the design and, thus, determined what would count as a good computer.

According to the strange cosmology of Aquinas's day, the second-order causes that determined which species of plants and animals there should be reproducing themselves in the world, what designs the terrestrial computers would have, were the 'heavenly bodies'. In some unexplained way the sun and the stars, circling the heavens with an absolute regularity (like the later laws of physics), were supposed to be at the origin of species. This determined that a giraffe would be generated in the image of its parents (its *first*-order cause – the immediately preceding computer) and, at another level, by the sun, its *second*-order cause. It is because of the second-order causal action of the sun that the first-order actions of the parents produce another identical giraffe, just as, in our example, it is the second-order action of the manufacturer which brings it about that the action of the computer brings about the next, identical computer in the series. All this appeal to the 'heavenly bodies' was simply the ancient attempt to explain the origin of species. A better answer to the same problem was provided by Charles Darwin, who noted that the offspring were sometimes (by chance mutation) *not* exactly identical with their parents and that, in some rare cases, this gave them an advantage in changed circumstances. This meant they lived longer and had more offspring identical with themselves than other, less advantaged relatives had, and finally outbred them. We should notice that the difference between Aquinas in the thirteenth century and Darwin in the nineteenth is entirely within the study of biology and need have no theological significance. The Christians who become hot under the theological collar about Darwin are those who do not think that God can creatively bring about random or chance or free occurrences, and who also hold that the first chapter of Genesis answers questions in biology and cosmology. Aquinas and his brethren, for the most part, would not accept either of these premises.

Anything made, then, in Aquinas's way of thinking, of its nature (because it is this kind of thing) tends toward or aims at what is intended *for* it by its *second-order cause*. In the case of living things that move themselves this is an active tendency and, in the case of animals, an appetite, a desire. Thus Aquinas says that each thing aims at, or has by nature an appetite for, its own perfection and good, and this perfection is to be found in the intention of the maker, which determined that it shall have that nature. In seeking its own perfection it is, *eo ipso*, seeking what is in the intention of the maker. In being attracted to its own perfection it is being attracted to its maker precisely as its maker, as having *that* intention.

Thus, for this Aristotelian thinking, the notion of good (aim or final cause) and the notion of efficient, explanatory cause come together. For Aquinas, Kant's dichotomy between truth and value is nonsensical. The good is the object of tendency and, in the case of higher animals, of appetite or desire. What it is that things tend towards is due to (and to be found in) their makers. To be a second-order maker is, as such, to be desired by what it has made as the thing made desires its own perfection. And, with all this in mind, and since God is the ultimate nth-order maker of everything, Aquinas concludes that each thing, in seeking its own perfection, is seeking (is oriented towards) God. In explaining the activity of any substance we need to look not only at the first-order cause (e.g. the parents of the giraffe, whose activity results in there being another individual of the species), nor simply at the second-order cause (e.g. the stars or the process of evolution) which determined that there should be *this* species instead of some other, but ultimately the cause in virtue of which there is anything instead of there not being anything, not the origin of the species but the origin of the origin of the species, the cause which Aquinas says we all call God.

So God is the ultimate maker, and, as such, the ultimately desirable, the ultimate good. Every creature, just in naturally tending to its own goodness, is seeking God as what ultimately intends it, as its maker. And this is what, for Aquinas, the goodness of God is first of all about: it is the goodness, the attractiveness or desirability inseparable from being Creator. God is the *omega* because he is the *alpha*, the end because he is the beginning. God is good because he is Creator; not, first, in the moral sense that it was very good of him to create us and we should be grateful, but in the metaphysical sense that, being Creator, he must be the ultimate object of our desire, without which we would have no desires. Aquinas puts this by saying that each creature tends to its own natural perfection, but God 'contains the perfections of all things', meaning not that he *is* all things, but that, as maker, he intends their perfections. God has these perfections, says Aquinas, 'in a higher way', in the way that they are in the intention of the *maker* before they are in the *thing made* – not before in time but in the sense that the presence of these perfections in the made things *depends on* them being in the intention of the maker.

It is because the Creator necessarily contains in this higher way all the perfections that are desired by creatures that we can apply to God words that signify such perfections. Thus we can say that God is wise because he contains (in a higher way) the wisdom that he has intended and created amongst creatures. Just because the wisdom exists in God in a higher way it exceeds what can be signified by our word 'wisdom', and thus, although we know there is wisdom in God, we cannot understand what it is like for God to be wise – in the way we *can* understand what it is like for Solomon or me to be wise. Aquinas points out that words like 'wise' are used quite literally of God. They are not used metaphorically. We mean that it is quite true that God is wise and quite *untrue that he is not* wise. Nevertheless, although used literally, these terms are used 'analogically', rather as, say, the word 'love' is used analogically when you say you love wine and you love your mother. The important difference, however, is that whereas we understand just as easily *both* the analogically related uses of 'love' in this case, we do not understand what the word 'good' or 'wise' refers to when it is used analogically of God.

Aquinas points out that not all words signifying perfections can be applied in this literal (though analogical) way to God, for many of them signify perfection within a context of creatureliness, or even of imperfection. Thus it is a perfection in human beings to be courageous or, in appropriate circumstances, sorrowful and contrite. To say of people that they are courageous is to presuppose that they encounter enemies or dangers, and obviously God cannot literally be threatened like that. So if we were to use such a word of God we would be speaking metaphorically, not literally. And a mark of this would be that it would be quite legitimate both to assert that God is courageous and to deny it – something that would be nonsense if we were speaking literally. Similarly, we must be speaking metaphorically if we say, as one of the authors of Genesis says, 'the Lord was sorry that he had made humankind' (Gen. 6.6).

It will now, perhaps, be clear why Aquinas thinks that we can apply to God words like 'just' and 'truthful' and 'merciful', which among us signify moral virtue, human virtue, without thereby intending to say that God is in our sense morally good. Such words (which do not have in their meaning any necessary reference to creaturely limitation) can be used of God literally. But because the perfections exist in him in a higher way than in us (for he is the Creator of our justice and our mercy, and so on), we can only use them analogically, recognizing that we do not understand the justice of God or comprehend the mystery of his mercy.

Nevertheless, to speak of the justice or the mercy of God, however incomprehensible it may be, does seem to qualify God's *activity*. It is hard to see how justice could belong (even in a higher way) to what has no activity at all. There is, however, a problem about God's activity and, in particular, God's voluntary activity – for, surely, only activities which are in some sense voluntary can be in any sense just or merciful.

I think that it never makes any sense to say that God might not have been what he actually is. There could be no potentiality in God, no 'what he might have been but is not'. Now this seems to exclude voluntary activity from God, for a voluntary act seems to be one which an agent might not have done had he or she chosen otherwise. Pagan neo-Platonists saw the world as a necessary emanation from God – given his nature and goodness (*bonum est diffusivum sui*). For Jews, and hence Christians, however, creation was an act of love, hence a voluntary act. God might not have been Creator, and yet he actually is. How can this be?

In dealing with this problem Aquinas distinguishes between different kinds of predicates used of God. Some, particularly those implying change or temporality, are applied to God not because of *his* nature, but because of what is the case about *other* things. So, on the one hand, we say that God is wise as one way of speaking about his nature, for God *is* his wisdom. And thus there could be no occasion when God is not wise. But, on the other hand, if we say God saved the soul of Peter, what we say was clearly not true before Peter existed or stood in need of salvation. Thus we are able to say that God became the saviour of Peter's soul. But, says Aquinas, these new predications become true not because of any change in God, but because of a change in *Peter*, of a (sort of) change in the whole universe. I say 'sort of' because, of course, creation is not a change – without it there is nothing to change. This depends on Aquinas's view that activity does not of itself necessarily involve a change in the agent, but only in the subject of the change. Thus, I can be said to teach you if and *only* if because of me a certain change – enlightenment, learning – takes place in you. Whatever energetic activities and changes take place in me, however much I talk or write or gesture or shout, however many hours I spend polishing my lectures, the activity of teaching has not occurred unless there is a change in you. It is merely a limiting condition of my nature that I can only bring about this change in you by, as a matter of fact, changing myself, working at it. There is nothing in the notion of teaching itself that involves such an effort and sweat in the teacher. There is thus no logical reason why God should not teach you or create you by bringing about something in you without in any way changing himself. In such a case there is a change in the relational propositions we can truly assert about God, but these new true propositions are founded in what happens to us, not in anything happening to God – as a tree which was at first on my right can be truly said to be now on my left without any change in the tree itself.

The corollary of this is that, though God is what he is necessarily and from eternity (there is nothing that he is that he might not have been), nevertheless there are things that he has done that, from the point of view of creatures, he might not have done – not because God might have been different, but because the subjects of his action might have been differently related to God. Peter's soul might not have been saved (if, for example, like St Philomena, Peter had never existed), and hence God might not have been truly called the saviour of Peter's soul.

Thus, the fact that God exists necessarily and that with him, as the Bible puts it, there is 'no variation or shadow due to change' (Jas 1.17), does not entail that the creation or anything within it necessarily happened. We can intelligibly say that God in unchanging eternity freely chose to save Peter's soul at the time when the contingent fact of Peter's soul being saved occurred. But this temporal action was the playing out in time of a will which is unchangeable and from eternity.

We can say that from eternity God willed that Peter should be saved in the twentieth century. But it is only in the twentieth century, and from then on, that we can call God 'saviour of Peter', not in the eighteenth or nineteenth century; so we can say that God *became* saviour of Peter – as, of course, we can say that, in Jesus, God became man (without there being thereby a change in God). Indeed, God became man in order that by having also a human nature God might be able to change, to suffer, to die.

It follows, of course, that for Aquinas, God cannot change his mind or be motivated to act by anything that happens amongst creatures. It cannot be true that God has decided to save Peter and that he has so decided because of what Peter has done (because he has repented, for example). It can, however, be true from eternity that God has decided to save Peter because of his repentance (that is how he shall be saved), just as he has decided from eternity to boil the kettle because of the fire underneath it (that is how it shall be boiled). The notion of petitionary prayer is unintelligible if we interpret it as putting pressure on God or seeking to *change his mind*. It is intelligible if we see it as the means God has chosen from eternity to bring about some outcome. Aquinas reminds us that my freely uttered prayer is as much a creature of God as is the 'answer' to my prayer. My prayer does not bring it about that God does something; God brings it about that it is my prayer that does something.

We can, then, speak of God's voluntary actions. We can speak of him as doing things that he might not have done. And so the stage is set for the problem of evil. If God might have made a world different from the one we live in, why did he not do so? Is he the voluntary cause of evil and misery in the world? And, if so, what content is there left to notions like God's justice and mercy? These are serious questions, but ones which would take me beyond what I want to say in the present essay.

9

Soul, Life, Machines and Language

I

Christians are sometimes thought to believe that people have souls rather in the way that others believe in Father Christmas or in fairies at the bottom of the garden. I mean, souls are thought to be extra entities besides what are recognized by other, perhaps more sceptical and tough-minded, people. We all know about bodies, but Christians are thought to tell us that, besides the visible bodies that we can scientifically examine, there are other, invisible things called souls – more or less loosely attached to these bodies.

The great thing about these souls (Christians are thought to believe) is that, being invisible and non-bodily, they are not subject to ordinary physical processes. In particular, they are not subject to decay and death. When the body dies, its soul just carries on unaffected – or even improved by being liberated from the prison of the body. Belief in souls is thought to be closely linked with wishful thinking about death. We don't want to believe that we simply go out of existence at death, so we imagine this immortal soul that cannot be destroyed.

The soul too is thought to have something to do with all those values of which the cynical scientific outlook of our culture takes no account. It fills a gap that is left in our way of articulating the world. In one way, to talk of souls is to indicate a sense of the inadequacy of our materialistic outlook. People sometimes shake their heads sadly and say how they would like to believe we have souls (as they might like to believe in fairies or God), but the harsh reality is that there are only chemicals and electromagnetic fields.

Souls are also thought to have something special to do with an interior and private life – a life that we can hide away from the public world. Many people think that they know directly about their own souls (you *just know* that you are doing soulish things, like thinking and feeling and loving, and so on) but cannot really be sure of anybody else's soul. There might just be me with my soul and, so far as the rest of the world goes, just bodies or machines with no souls hidden inside. For these people, souls are much the same as minds (they make the same mistakes about both).

Because souls are thought to be private and interior, those Christians who talk about souls are thought to be the kind who would restrict the scope of the gospel to our private and interior lives. There are, as you know, Christians who think that the gospel has nothing to say about public, political and social matters but is exclusively concerned with the interior life of the individual, with 'what we do with our solitude'. These Christians are said to think that the gospel is not about, say, poverty and liberation, but about 'saving our souls'. We consist of two bits: a body and a soul. The body has to do with the public world, with science and with the realm of Caesar which passes away; the soul has to do with privacy, with values and with the realm of God, which does not pass away.

I think that all this jumble of ideas is what people commonly associate with the word 'soul'. And, all this being so, it is quite probable that we ought to abandon the word 'soul' altogether when we are doing theology or philosophy. Indeed, some years ago I produced a short introduction to Catholic thinking, a catechism, in which I was most careful to avoid the word 'soul' because I thought it could only mislead people in these ways.[1]

---

[1] Herbert McCabe OP, *The Teaching of the Catholic Church: A New Catechism of Christian Doctrine* (London: Darton, Longman, Todd, 2000).

If you are interested in the quite important things that classical
or medieval thinkers were bothered about when they discussed
psyche or *anima*, if you share the puzzles that they were trying
to cope with, it is perhaps of no help at all to talk about souls.

II

So let us begin where Aristotle very sensibly began: to ask
about the soul is to ask about what we mean when we say that
something is *alive*. To discuss the soul is to discuss *life*. I take
this as the starting-point because I think this is what traditional
Christian thinkers took as their starting-point. When they considered God and the soul they did not think first of God and
human minds, or of God and private experiences, religious or
otherwise, or of 'God and the conscious self'; they thought of
God and being alive. Usually they would be interested mainly
in God and being humanly alive, or God and human existence,
as we might say nowadays. And for the strand of Christian tradition in which I was brought up, in order to understand human
living we need to see it in the context of animal life in general
and, indeed, of organic life in general. So that is what I propose
to do. What do we mean when we distinguish the animate from
the inanimate – animals, let us say, from machines or stones?

Life, says Thomas Aquinas, is essentially that by which anything has power to move itself – taking movement in its wide
sense.[2] 'Life' is a word used in several different, but related,
senses. It does not mean the same thing to say that a buttercup
is alive and that a tiger is alive, but it is not by a mere acci-
dent of the English language, or a pun, that we use the same
word 'alive' in both cases. 'Alive' is used, as Aquinas would
say, analogically, just as 'love' is used analogically in 'I love a
good rare steak' and 'I love my country'. In every case, though,

---

[2]Cf. *Summa Theologiae*, Ia, 18, 1 and 18, 2.

at whatever level we are using the word 'life', we are speaking of what at some level has the power to move *itself*, not just to be at the mercy of others. In this tradition living things are automobiles, self-movers. And in this tradition *anima* or 'soul' (which is also, of course, used analogically) means being, at some level, able to move oneself. All automobiles, at whatever level, have souls, at some level of the word 'soul'. So in this way of talking, potatoes and cockroaches have souls. This does not mean that potatoes and cockroaches have an elementary form of consciousness or an elementary form of what is to evolve into human consciousness. To say, in the traditional manner, that cockroaches have souls is not to say that they have feelings rather like us, or that they have 'animal rights'. It is just to say that they are living things, unlike, say, lumps of lead or tape recorders. Cockroaches are self-moving in a sense that tape recorders are not. They are not self-moving in the sense that *I* am, for in my case self-moving has reached the very high level of freedom and creativity, of being responsible for my actions and character, but they are self-moving all the same. So cockroaches are alive; cockroaches have souls because they are automobiles. So it is time we thought about cars.

Most people do not think that cars are alive. Most people draw a sharp distinction between cars and cockroaches. Now is this blind prejudice? Why should *these* automobiles be arbitrarily excluded from the realm of living things – and, while we are on about it, what about computers? Or is it just that we have it wrong; perhaps being alive is *not* to do with being automobile? Here I come down on the side of saying that cars are not alive because they are not truly auto-mobile (automobiles are not automobiles, just as God isn't a god). Let us see why.

All living things that are self-moving, at least in the sense of moving physically, must be complex. They have to be made up of parts so that when one part moves another the whole thing moves the whole thing. A leopard is self-moving because the action of one part of it, the brain, which is an action of the leopard, moves another part of it, the legs, which is a move-ment of the leopard. So it is an action of the leopard (using its brain) that causes a movement of the leopard (using its legs). It is leopard moving leopard. It is self-moving. Now all this de-pends on both brain and legs being *parts* of the leopard, so that an action of the brain is not just an action of this lump of grey matter but also an action of the whole leopard; and similarly with the movement of the legs. This implies that if you ampu-tated the leopard's leg, separated it from the whole to which it belongs, it would become a different thing altogether. Before the amputation, if you were so ill advised as to punch the leop-ard's leg you would simply be punching the leopard. That is *what it is* that you would be punching. After the amputation you would not only not be punching a *leopard*, you would not even be punching a *leg*. A detached leg is not a kind of leg, as a dead cow is not a kind of cow, or a forged banknote is not a kind of banknote. And this is not just because we mean by the *word* 'leg' something that is a functioning organ of the animal. It is because in the living beast the leg *is* a functioning organ of the animal. It is because we think the leopard is self-moving and thus a living thing. It is because we do *not* think that the wheels of a car are, in this sense, essentially functioning organs of the car that we do not think that a car is alive. I mean that we think of the leopard as the natural unit of which the legs and the brain are essentially parts; being a part-of-the-leopard is what it is for the leg to be what it is; it has the existence as what it now is by being a part-of-the-leopard. The whole leopard, so to say, comes first. The parts are secondary – if the leg ceases to be part of the leopard it will turn into something completely different – as mutton is something completely dif-ferent from a sheep. So a leopard is alive because it has organs which exist as what they are precisely *by* being organs, being functioning parts of a prior whole.

Now the reason why we do not think a car is alive is, I think, because we assemble a car from bits which already exist as what they are; and we do not think they turn into something completely different by becoming parts of the car. They are not parts of the car in the sense that legs are parts of a leopard. In this case the bits are prior to the car. One striking illustration of this is that while we can dismember a leopard by taking the bits apart, we cannot assemble a leopard simply by adding the bits together. But a car is secondary; it is simply an assemblage of already existing things that have been put in contact with each other. The units in this case are the bits, and the car is only a quasi-unit by courtesy of our construction and our culture and our language. It is because this is what we think about cars that we think they are not alive. If you belonged to a primitive and blessed community that had no cars, and thus if you knew nothing about how cars are assembled from bits, and if you came across one for the first time, you would almost certainly think it was alive. When you learnt more about it you would realize that it is not. What you would learn is that the car is not really a natural unit but only a quasi-unit, so that you cannot say literally that the wheels are *organs* of the car. They just act *as though* they were organs of the car; the car is an imitation animal with imitation organs. It is just because the engine is not literally an organ that the action of the engine is not literally an action of the whole car, so that when the engine moves the wheels it is not literally the whole car moving the whole car. It is not literally a case of automobility. It is one thing, the engine, moving another thing, the wheels, with which it happens to be in contact (of course neither the engine nor the wheels are natural units either: they are themselves quasi-units constructed from more primitive natural substances).

III

Now of course, the whole of this account depends on accepting the idea of 'natural units' as distinct from quasi-units that are assembled from them. Yet this is the way that we do *in fact* think and talk. We talk as though we are familiar with natural units. Although we talk metaphorically of the 'life' of a city, we do not think that a city is literally alive, precisely because we do not think a city is a natural unit. We can for many purposes treat it as though it were a unit, but we realize that fundamentally it is an assemblage of all kinds of things that exist in their own right prior to becoming parts of the city. Indeed, we continually recognize that there are natural units and quasi-units, that some of the things we name by single nouns or noun phrases are assemblages and others are natural units. For example, what is named by the phrase 'a human being' is a natural unit, but a human being who is employed to deliver the mail, what is named by the word 'postman', is not a natural unity, but an assemblage of being a human being plus having a particular job. Someone who could not find any significant difference between someone ceasing to be a postman by changing his job (the disintegration of a quasi-unit) and someone ceasing to be a human being by dying (the disintegration of a natural unit) would strike us as intellectually very different from us.

I do not know how to give an account of the way we have come to divide up our experienced world into natural kinds or natural units; it is evidently an extremely important part of the business of living with things and interacting with them in all sorts of ways. It has to do with what we might call 'practices'. It seems to me that the idea that we are completely free to reclassify the objects of experience in just any way at all, or (what is the same thing) to use just any names at all to express what it is to be a unit in our world, rests on the idea that we are simply spectators of something that stands over against us called 'the world' and we are at liberty to put just any kind of grid we like between the world and our eyes. In fact we are not just spectators, we are involved with and have to cope with things. And recognizing the natural units is part of coping.

So one of the things we have in mind when we say that cockroaches are natural units, and thus alive, in the way that cars are not natural units, is that cockroaches are, and have been, natural units quite regardless of ourselves. There were cockroaches busy being individual natural units before humankind evolved, and, I am told, they will probably go on after we have blown ourselves to bits. Cars evidently have to be assembled by us; cockroaches do not.

But what about synthetic life? Quite apart from genetic engineering, could we not assemble a car complicated enough to be living? We already have computer-controlled cars which do not need a driver. They can detect roadways and obstacles and cope with other traffic by themselves. It would be a small thing for them to have a mechanism by which they would seek out and collect their own petrol, and so on. There seems no reason in principle why such a machine should not be able to collect together the necessary materials and construct exact reproductions of itself, which of course would then set about making reproductions in their turn, just as it is with DNA molecules. We would then have a machine which could move around, feed itself and reproduce itself. Would we not say that it was alive? I think we quite probably would. We could claim to have synthesized life. But notice that we would only be inclined to say it was alive just to the extent that it does *not* need to be synthesized; to the extent that it has an ancestry rather than a manufacturer; to the extent that it *does* reproduce itself independently of us; to the extent that it is no longer an artefact but is self-moving and self-reproducing and lives a life of its own. And this, I think, shows that we were right to contrast being alive and being assembled by others. Even if we did assemble such a machine in the first place, we could regard its successors as alive just in so far as they no longer need us and escape from our control. We might, incidentally, expect such a synthesized life which is not produced within the balance of a whole evolutionary system to be a danger to the ecological

130

structure on which it intrudes. I have even heard it suggested that the AIDS virus was originally just such an artificial life-form, an unintended spin-off of genetic engineering. But that may be just science fiction.

In any living thing, then, whether natural or (hypothetically) synthetic, the basic characteristic is that it is not an assemblage of prior parts but rather that its parts are organs of it, take their meaning from being parts of it, and do not exist as what they now are before or after being parts of it.

I have just used the word 'meaning', and this was deliberate. For it is with organic structures that we first encounter meaning or significance, which is a certain kind of relationship of part to whole.

Let me repeat that an organic structure is one in which the whole is prior to the parts, so that we give an account of the parts by reference to the whole, and not vice versa. It is the account of the whole that is what it took for a thing to be in the first place. When you are confronted by a car, 'what it took for all this to be in the first place' is given by speaking of all the various bits that were assembled. The car itself is only the configuration of things that were already established as what they were. When, however, you are confronted by a cockroach, 'what it took for all this to be in the first place' is given by an account of the whole cockroach; to consider any one of the bits in isolation is to look at it in the abstract, in abstraction from the whole to which it belongs.

It is characteristic of organic structures that the parts, the organs, exist at two levels, and this is expressed by the fact that there are two levels of language at which to speak of them. What I mean is that you can, for example, talk of a leg in abstraction from the whole body; you can consider its muscles and nerves, and so on, and how they operate. Or again you can talk about the leg as an organ, as having a function within the whole body, as, for example, that by which the animal *walks*. Similarly, you can consider the eyeball and what it does and what happens to it in terms of lenses and the retina and electric impulses; or again you can see it as an organ of sight, which is to see the relevance of its operation to the whole body. To say that an animal *sees* with its eyes is to say that what happens in the eye is relevant to, makes a difference to, has significance for, the whole body. The way to tell whether an animal is sighted or not is to find out whether its total behaviour is any different in the dark from in the light. Seeing is an operation done with the eye, but it is an operation of the entire body. So the eye has an operation of its own which is itself *also* an operation of the entire body. That is what I meant by saying that an organ exists at two levels, and that this is expressed by talking about it at two levels. The eye does not undergo electrochemical changes and *also* do something else which is seeing; its sight just is its physiological modification as *meaningful* for the whole animal.

With non-organic structures we can also have two levels of talking about the parts. We can consider the car's engine in terms of its internal combustion, its petrol consumption, and so on, or we can talk about it as what makes the car go, its relevance to the behaviour of the whole machine. But in this case the engine does not exist at two levels. We just talk of it as though it did, just as we talk of the whole machine as though it were a whole, a unit, when in fact it is simply an assemblage of bits. A machine, as I have said, is an imitation animal; so it is convenient to talk of it in organic, animal terms.

Another way of putting this is to say that in an organic structure each of the organs has both an operation and a meaning to its operation. The meaning of the operation of the eye or the heart or the leg is the part it plays in the structure of the whole language. When we talk of the operation of the eye with reference to the operation of the whole animal, when we talk of it as seeing, when we talk of it as meaningful for the whole structure, we are talking of it as a *vital* operation, as part of the life of the whole animal. Another way of putting this is to say that seeing is an operation of the soul.

When we talk like that we are in some danger of thinking of the soul as another organ alongside the eye and the hand, and so on. This temptation is to be resisted. To say that seeing is an operation of the soul is just to say that it is the operation of the organ, the eye, precisely as an organ, that is, as meaningful for the whole body, for the life of the animal. What happens in the eyeball is meaningful for the animal when because of it the animal does something – it runs away, for example, or pounces, or whatever. All the organs of sense are bits of the body which, when they are affected, make the world meaningful for the animal; because of them the animal responds in appropriate ways to its environment, now recognized as significant for it. It is because the organs are themselves significant parts of the whole body that what affects them is taken up into the structure of the whole body and is thus meaningful. The photoelectric effects on the retina of the eye are *sensations* because the eye is a functional part of a complex structure.

IV

So a living body, a body with a soul, is one in which not only *events* happen but *meaningful* events. If I shine a red light on a white cat it will turn red, or at least pink, and the redness will be simply the cat's colour; but if I shine it in its eyes, just because its eyes are organs it will be a *sensation*, a factor in making the cat's world significant to it. The redness will be in the cat's fur simply naturally, as it would be on any reddish surface; but if the light shines in the eye the redness will be in the cat, as Aquinas would say, 'intentionally', as a factor in the cat's interpretation of the world. In other words, we are here at the beginnings of awareness, or knowledge. The cat is not just reddened, it has a sensation of red, it is aware of redness. In fact I am not at all sure that a cat would be affected by redness (for all I know, cats might be colour-blind). But the same story can be told with, say, the smell of a mouse. There is a great deal of difference between a cat beginning to smell like a mouse because the mouse has foolishly snuggled up against it, and the smell reaching the nostrils of the cat, which are organs. Then the smell becomes a sensation, part of the pattern of the cat's vital activities and tendencies to action.

If you have a magnetic needle it will *tend* to point to magnetic north; it will do so unless prevented. This is because of a characteristic the magnetic needle has, a certain alignment of some of its molecules. Now it belongs to animals such as cats that they have tendencies not only because of characteristics that they naturally have (like the tendency to fall if you let go of them because they are naturally heavier than air) but also because of characteristics that they have 'intentionally', sensations that they receive. So the cat will have a tendency to pounce because it *smells* a mouse (it has the smell of the mouse intentionally), or because it *sees* or *hears* its movements (it has the appearance of the mouse intentionally). In these cases the movement of the mouse and the movement of the cat are mediated by sensations, by awareness, by the cat having a sensuous interpretation of its world. It moves because of what the world *means* to it.

To say this is to suggest that talk of a stimulus 'triggering' the response of the cat is misleading because it oversimplifies the situation. The metaphor of the pressure on the trigger making the gun fire won't do here because the effect of the stimulus is to produce not a movement but a *tendency* to move. The stimulus enters into a whole pattern of other stimuli; the tendency it produces becomes part of a balance of other stimuli, and the outcome is therefore nothing like as predictable as would be the case with a trigger and an explosion. Pavlovian experiments to make dogs predictably salivate, or whatever, work by artificially placing the animal in conditions in which other responses are ruled out. This is, of course, the correct procedure if you are, for example, investigating the effect of introducing an extra methyl radical into an organic molecule, or the precise effect of decreased moisture on the biological ageing of a plant. Your experimental aim is to eliminate other processes and reactions and look at this particular one in isolation. But if you look at animal behaviour with these same techniques it is not surprising if you get results which suggest that the animal is nothing other than a machine. The experiment is, so to say, rigged to treat it as a machine. The animal's *not* being a machine is nothing other than the fact that its whole experience, the very many complex stimuli it is receiving, ought to be taken into account together if you want to give a correct account of it. The animal is a whole which is prior to its parts, and to treat its parts in isolation (though illuminating for many purposes) is to abstract from the full truth about the animal.

To say, then, that the cat 'has a soul' or 'has life' is not to say that there is an extra invisible organ or an 'entelechy' that the Pavlovian behaviourist has overlooked. It is not to add to the description of the cat; it is to say what sort of descriptions are appropriate to it; it is to say what sort of being a cat is; it is to say 'what it takes for it to be a cat' in the first place. It is to say which sort of investigative techniques are appropriate to it and which are merely dealing with abstractions from the total reality.

If you decide that a cat is such a living animal (and this does seem the common-sense thing to decide) then you can make sense of saying that the cat has experiences and sensations and, moreover, that it has memory and can learn – that it can do things willingly or unwillingly, that it can suffer and search and try to do things and recognize itself over against its world. None of these things can literally be said of machines; and none of these things necessarily entail having what people call a human consciousness.

V

I want to move from these considerations to looking at the human animal, at the *human* soul. But first it will be necessary to look at the individual animal as a member of a species.

Just as each part of an animal is an organ, a functioning part of the whole body, so there is a sense in which each individual animal is itself a kind of organ, a functioning part of its species. And let us be clear that when we speak of an animal species we are not speaking of some kind of logical classification. The species *dog* is not the class of all animals which resemble each other in certain respects. The species is an historical or material entity, or at least a material entity extending through time. By the species to which a dog belongs I mean its ancestry and its progeny. There is a physical and not just a conceptual connection between all dogs; they are genetically and not merely logically related.

I shall be comparing and contrasting the way that an individual animal belongs to, is part of, a species, its genetic community, and the way that the human animal belongs to a culture, its linguistic community. I shall be suggesting that to have symbols and words is to have a particular way of belonging to a community, rather as having genes is to have another way of belonging to a community.

I say that an individual dog is in a sense an organ of the dog species because there is a sense in which, just as the whole animal is prior to its parts, so the species is prior to the individual, and the individual can most properly be understood as a part of the species. A logical class, by contrast, is secondary to its members and exists only in function of them. That is one reason why we can invent any classifications we like. As a mere classificatory device there is no more reason to class all dogs together than to class all hairy things or all two-eyed things together, or all the animals I noticed on Thursday. But a dog has to be born of other members of the species, and much of its behaviour is intelligible only as a functioning part of this species, as that by which the species is perpetuated.

Animals arrive equipped genetically with a whole lot of behavioural tendencies; they do not have to learn to take flight or to attack in the face of certain dangers; they do not have to learn to be sexually attracted to other members of their species or to make preparation for rearing their young. All these tendencies are genetically supplied, supplied by the species; and if they were not, the species would not survive. Just as we can see teeth and claws as organs by which the individual survives, so we might see the individual as a kind of organ by which the genes survive. This explains what is sometimes called the 'altruistic' behaviour of animals. In the defence of their young they may sacrifice their lives, transcending their individual self-preservation for the sake of species preservation. It is natural for us to speak metaphorically of such behaviour in moral language because there is some sort of analogy between, on the one hand, the interaction of individual animals and their genetic community and, on the other, the dialectical interaction of the individual human animal and its genetico-cultural community, which is the starting-point of ethics. That is why ethics is related to, but immensely more interesting than, ethology.

The genetic determinants of animal behaviour do of course change with changes in their natural environment, but only by the cumbersome mechanism of natural selection. The cultural demands upon the linguistic animal change with enormously greater rapidity. We have history instead of evolution, and we have the handing-on of acquired characteristics that we call *tradition*. In the evolutionary process, the slightest variation requires a generation. Yet we can change culturally within our lifetimes – every time we are convinced by an argument or converted to a new way of life, or conduct or endure a revolution of any kind. All this comes about by the use of symbols and the systems of symbols that we can broadly call 'language'. It is because of language that we are alive in a different way from other animals; and it is because of language that we are self-transcendent in a different way from other animals.

Let us take a look at symbols. As I have said, there is a difference between shining a red light on the fur of an animal and shining it in its eyes simply because the eyes are a particular kind of organ. In the one case, the redness is in the animal as a pink colour on its surface; in the other, it is present as a sensation, 'intentionally' present as part of the animal's interpretation of its world. What this intentional presence amounts to is that the sensation plays a part in the animal's response to its world, its tendency to behave. Now this is to oversimplify; something like a sheep may not respond to red lights or sensations of red – that is only one tiny element in the delivery of all its sensations and the memory of previous sensations (for the more complex animals can retain the sensation of what it was like to be sensed in the past). And all this is blended with genetically determined tendencies. So it is merely schematic and a bit absurd to speak of a sensation offered in isolation.

Let us then think rather of the sheep's recognition of a chunk of its environment (a wolf, say) as dangerous and to be avoided. This is the combination of a great many present sensations, memories and instincts.

The dangerousness of the wolf exists in one way in the wolf (it *is* as a matter of fact dangerous to sheep) and in another way in the sense-structure of the sheep. It is *perceived* as dangerous; the danger exists intentionally in the sheep. When the dangerousness of the wolf impinges on the sheep, the sheep does not become dangerous, just as when the red light enters its eyes they do not become red or pink (as the fleece would). The dangerousness is present in the sheep intentionally, and this amounts to certain behavioural tendencies – like running away. The sheep is acting as though *this* chunk of its environment had a certain meaning for it, a significance for its own life. The dangerousness which in the wolf is a mere natural characteristic of it becomes, in the nervous system of the sheep, a *meaning*; a motive, for example, for action. We rightly say: the sheep ran away because it perceived the wolf and perceived it as dangerous.

Now what I want to stress here is that it is the same dangerousness, what Aristotle or Aquinas would call the same *form*, that is present in one way in the wolf itself and in another way in the nervous system and brain of the sheep. In the former case it is present as an account of what the wolf *is in fact* like. In the latter case it is present as *playing its part* in a structure of vital behaviour. It is the *same* form, that is, if the sheep is in a healthy state, if it is seeing the world normally, if it is in a state to survive. There might be a confused sheep which saw grass as dangerous and wolves as edible, but it would not live long. Ordinarily it is the *same* form that is objectively or naturally in the thing perceived and intentionally in the perceiver, as a perception. So it is the same form that could be an account of what is the case in the material world and also an account of what is going on in the nervous system of the sheep. In the nervous system it exists as a *meaning*, as part of a structure as relating to other parts of that structure, what happens in the sheep's eyes and nose as relevant to what it does with its feet. Notice that the dangerousness which was a simple physical *fact* in the wolf has now become a kind of meta-fact, a second-order fact, a matter of the *relevance* of what is happening in one organ to the whole organism. The dangerousness in the wolf is made of bone and tooth and muscle; as a perception it is made of relevance. The perception is not itself a physical object, it is the relations of one physical object to others. It exists at a certain level of abstraction. Aquinas did not hesitate to say that the perceptions of animals are 'spiritual', meaning that an animal acts in terms of such meta-fact relations of relevance and not simply as, say, a billiard ball is pushed physically by another.[3]

[3]Cf. ibid., Ia, 72, 1.

Of course, and as I have noted, if you want to you can treat an animal for some purposes as a machine and analyse its movements in billiard-ball terms. Except as a methodological device for treating some problem in abstraction, however, that would be perverse. It would be to treat an animal as an imitation animal. It is part of what we mean when we say that it *is* an animal (that it is alive) that it is an organism and that its behaviour is to be spoken of in terms of meanings and relevance.

For an animal to perceive a form (a 'what things are like') is for this form to be taken up into the structure of the animal's body as a matter of the relevance of an organ to the whole organism. And I am now going to suggest that for a human animal to have a form as a thought is roughly speaking for this form to be taken up into the structure of language as a matter of the relevance of a symbol to the whole language. The meaning of any word is the part it plays in, its relevance to, the whole language; to be able to use a word is to have a form in mind, to be able to have a thought. To have a mind is to be able to use such symbols.

That we use such symbols is quite simply a fact about human animals, and it seems to me the fundamental fact about them. It does not just make them into a different species of animal, as a giraffe is of a different species from a rabbit. It makes them into animals in a new sense (just as having sensations marks off giraffes from buttercups).

Human animals are animals in a new sense for this reason: other animals are organic bodily structures and, moreover, they belong organically to the greater structure which is the species; but the structures in question here are *given*. For any animal to be, to be alive, is for it to be structured in these particular ways. Within these structures the animal operates in terms of meanings – for meaning just *is* the relationship of *part* to *whole* in a *structure*. Now the human animal not only shares in much of this but it operates in structures that are *of its own making*. It is the special characteristic of the human animal that it operates in terms of structures, and thus of meanings, which are its own spontaneous creation. We are not born with language, we create it and learn it. Other animals are simply born with a repertoire of symbols.

I should like at this point, if I can, to scotch a red herring. I most certainly do not want to say that human animals are like other animals in all other respects but that unlike the others they also have this special game of playing with symbols or words. I am not saying that lots of animals can hunt and swim and make love but the human ones can talk *as well*. Quite the contrary: I am saying that pretty well all the behaviour of human animals is significantly different from that of other animals. And if you *analyse* this difference, you find it has to do with the human's ability to deploy symbols. I do not say that the characteristic human thing *is* the deployment of symbols.

Thus human animals can hunt intelligently or stupidly (and this is not the same as hunting well or badly). If you try to explain what you meant by saying that someone hunted intelligently you have to say something like: it was as though she were saying to herself, 'If I do so and so . . .' You are emphatically not saying that as a matter of psychological fact she *did* say these things to herself, as though acting intelligently were *both* acting *and* carrying on an internal monologue. Now what sort of thing do you mean by saying she acted *as though* she were saying, 'If I do so and so . . .'? An account of what she in fact *did* might not differ much from the account of a leopard cunningly hunting, just as the account of what the leopard did might not differ much from what a computerized machine might seem to do. What makes the difference between her and the leopard is that you describe her actions against the background of endless other possibilities that might have been. OK, she acted just like a leopard would have done, but the leopard *had* to act like that; a leopard that did not act like that would necessarily have been a sick or defective leopard. She might have acted differently without being sick or incompetent; she might have had very good reasons; she might have *wanted* to hunt badly – she might have been bribed to do so, or she might be doing it to take the mickey out of a lot of solemn people, or any one of an indefinite number of reasons. To say that she *has* reasons for acting is to say that it is as though she were saying certain things to herself. Of course there *is* a reason why the leopard hunts; he is a healthy leopard and he or his cubs are hungry; he acts for a reason; but the leopard does not *have* this reason. It is not one he proposes to himself; he just has a *significant* experience in virtue of his bodily structure. But to *propose* a reason to yourself you have to do something analogous to talking.

It is because the leopard cannot *analyse* its action in words (not just *does* not, but *cannot*) that, while it can act willingly or unwillingly, it cannot act intentionally, with an intention. The dog tearing away across the garden after the neighbour's cat is visibly acting voluntarily or willingly. You can see it and hear it barking with exuberance and joy. It is acting in accordance with its sensual structure of meaning. If you call it back, it will come back (if it is a well-trained dog), but it will be visibly reluctant and unwilling.

What is special about human animals is that we not only, like the dog, have things we like to do, things we are reluctant not to do. We can also formulate aims and intentions for ourselves. This formulation, or setting of aims for ourselves, can only be expressed by saying, 'We did what amounted to saying to ourselves: this is what I am trying to achieve, and this is how I will achieve it.' This is different from simply having an aim, in that you might not have formulated it or set it for yourself. It is just this 'is, but might not have been' that language exists to express. Whenever I act intentionally it is always possible for you to ask me, 'What did you do that for?' (meaning not exactly 'What did you hope to achieve by doing that?' but 'What was the meaning of your action?', 'What was it that your act was an act of?'). And whatever answer I give will be informative precisely because there might have been other answers. This is the one story and it might have continued differently. In the case of a dog's action, the question, 'What did it do that for?' is answered by an accurate account of what it did in the context of the kind of beast that it is and the circumstances – if you get this answer right there are no other possibilities. Other answers only remain possible in the sense that you might find out more about, say, the circumstances; whatever answer you *finally* come to renders all the others not only false but impossible. This is not so with human action.

VI

So for an adequate account of human activities it is necessary to refer to the intentions with which actions are done. To have an intention is to be able to answer the question, 'Why did you do that?' It is not necessary actually to ask and answer that question either with material words or by imagining the use of material words, but it is to be *prepared to*, to be able to, answer the question. Of course there are a lot of things I do for which I cannot answer such a question. I may scratch my chin and I may not only be unable to say why I did it – I might not even have noticed that I did it. Again, I undergo a whole series of operations like breathing and digesting food of which it would be senseless to ask why I did them. Still, there are also a lot of activities, and these ones we think of as characteristically human, of which we can sensibly ask: 'Why did you do that?' or 'What was that for?' or, for that matter, 'Why did you do nothing?' And this is to ask: Supposing you *had* actually said to yourself, 'I am going to do A and this is the way I will do it', what would 'A' have been? This means that questions about intentions only make sense in the case of animals *to whom* questions can be addressed.

You can certainly speak of the reason why the dog chased the cat. But asking the dog about it does not enter into the matter. This is not just because the dog happens to be dumb, but because, being non-linguistic, it cannot have its own reasons; it cannot have intentions – rather as, in a more extreme case, there is a reason why water flows downhill, but water does not *have* a reason for flowing downhill. An intention, then, seems to be a reason for action that is my own reason, something I propose to myself.

That is why intentional action is the most thorough kind of self-moving or, if you like, the highest kind of vitality, of life. The life or soul of the linguistic animal, the one that can have intentions, is the most lively kind of life, the highest kind of soul (the highest we have looked at so far, anyway).

I should say, by the way, that when I say that I can have my own reason in a way that a dog cannot have its own reason I am not claiming that my own intentions are always absolutely clear to me. I just mean that I can try to answer your question, 'Why did you do that?', whereas a dog cannot even attempt this. I may very well fail; it may very well happen that other people know more about my intentions than I do; it is quite common for me to conceal my true intentions from myself. I may very well tell myself loudly and clearly that I am acting from the highest possible principles and a cool sense of justice when everybody else knows I am acting out of resentment and wounded vanity. I am by no means the best authority on my intentions. Still, though, I can have intentions to be wrong or deceive myself about, and dogs cannot.

I hope I have been able to provide at least an intelligible sketch of the connection between being able to use symbols, and especially words, and having intentions and, thus, being self-moving or living in an especially intense way. My actions are *my* actions in a quite new and deeper way because I have language. Note, though, that the same connection can be made the other way round. I have language because my actions are my own in a special way. I want to say that the production of concepts (which are capacities to use symbols) is, and has to be, a free and spontaneous business. I have concepts because I am creative.

With non-linguistic animals (and for a lot of the time with linguistic animals) they cannot help having the *sensations* they have. In a way, the world imposes sensations on the animal. As I have already suggested, there are all sorts of nuances and qualifications to be made to this; the experience an animal will have in given circumstances will depend on a whole lot of other factors besides what is physically impinging on it here and now; but, still, the meaning of its world *imposes* itself on the animal. This is because the meaning of the world exists in the animal as a conformation of its nervous system including, of course, its brain. Just as the meaning of, say, the wolf (its being dangerous) exists in the wolf as a set of facts about its teeth and claws and what not, so this meaning exists in the sheep as a set of related facts about its nerves and brain, and about the relations between them. Given ordinary circumstances and ordinary healthy wolves and sheep, there is no way that the dangerousness that exists in the wolf physically will not exist *intentionally* in the nervous system of the sheep looking at it. Yet there is a dramatic difference when we come to consider how I might come to *talk* to myself or to others about the wolf. As it happens, I have never met a wolf socially, but I expect that when I do I shall feel at least as uneasy as a sheep does. Yet besides accommodating the dangerousness of the wolf in the structure of my nervous system I can also accommodate it in a different way in the structure of my language. Dangerousness exists in one way in the wolf itself; in another way in my sensual experience; in yet another way as the meaning of the word 'dangerous'.

The wolf is a material thing that has dangerousness; I have a material organic structure that experiences dangerousness; the words of the English language are material things that signify dangerousness. Now a vital difference between the experience and the signifying is that experience is what happens to me because of the material apparatus of my nervous system, but significance is the way I *use* the material things which are words or other symbols. Significance is in my use of the symbols; it is a matter of my creative activity. Experience, by comparison, is passive. This of course oversimplifies because experiencing and signifying are interwoven, and how I actually experience my world is culturally conditioned; it depends on how I talk of my world. Nevertheless it is one thing to use a microscope to see something more clearly and quite another to use language (in itself, equally material) to articulate the world more clearly. Microscopes function *because* of their material properties, words do not; they function as signs because of how we use them, their physical properties don't really matter. Of course this too is hopelessly oversimplified. Pretty well all poetry depends on the material properties of words, their sound and feel and music; and this is what makes poetry hard to translate. Nevertheless translation is possible, and translation from Serbo-Croat to Donegal Irish is possible because quite different material things can carry approximately or even exactly the same meanings.

The fact that the material things which are Serbo-Croat noises and the material things that are Donegal Irish noises can carry the same meaning does not entail that we can recognize some abstracted pure meaning that can happen to be carried by either of these vehicles. It is just that we recognize (somehow) that this word in this culture has the same or a similar function as that word in that culture. I do not see how we could *detach* the meaning of a word from the material word itself any more than you could detach, say, the dangerousness of a wolf from the material wolf itself. But there is nonetheless a difference here: although the *meaning* dangerousness cannot be detached from the material word 'dangerous' or some equivalent word: it does not depend on the material constitution of that word in the way that the dangerousness in the wolf depends on the material constitution of the wolf. You can do things to the material wolf to stop it having dangerousness. You can draw its fangs and clip its claws. Signs are not related to their meanings in *that* way. This is, of course, why physically completely different signs in different languages, or even the same languages, can have the same meanings.

We cannot understand a meaning without the use of material signs, but understanding is not a function of the material properties of the signs. (I am, of course, here regarding imagining that you are speaking as just as much a matter of physiological processes as actual speaking.) This comes close to, if it is not identical with, something that Aquinas often says: that understanding and thinking cannot take place naturally without a physiological process he calls *imaginatio*, but nevertheless understanding is not itself a physiological process.[4] I think that what he calls *imaginatio* may be rather like what later (Cartesian-style) philosophers called 'consciousness' and attached such importance to. Aquinas regards it as a great achievement of classical Greek philosophy to have distinguished understanding from this kind of consciousness: understanding is not any operation of bodily organs, although it cannot take place without such bodily operations.[5] This for him provides an explanation of why hangovers and operations on the brain may interfere with our thinking: an explanation which does not have recourse to the implausible view that thinking itself is an operation of the brain.

We have the sensations we have, broadly speaking, because of the structure of our nervous systems. We conceive the meanings we have not because of the physical structure of our words, or of our enunciation or imagining of words, but because of the use we make of these signs in the human business of

[4]Cf. ibid., Ia, 84, 7.
[5]Ibid., Ia, 84, 1.

communication with each other which lies at the heart of the human kind of society.

It seems to me quite plain that a human society is a structure in which the bits are related to the whole in ways quite unlike the way the bits of a typewriter are related to the machine, or the ways the organs of a body are related to the whole animal, or the ways that individual animals are related to a whole species. It seems to me plain that we create historically the ways in which we relate to each other. When I say it is 'quite plain' I mean that it does not seem to me that this is a theory any more than the view that daffodils die or tigers become enraged is a theory. I mean it is the kind of view that you need a theory in order to *deny*. I mean you *could* have a metaphysical theory according to which the only true knowledge is, say, physics or chemistry, and other sciences like botany, biology, sociology and psychology are either coded versions of chemistry, or else not knowledge at all. If you held that theory then you would have to explain how human society looks the way it does when in fact it is really quite different. But since there is no reason I can think of for having such a metaphysical theory, I think we can be spared this tedious chore. It just seems to be plainly the case that the symbols through which human communication and community are constituted, the culture of a community, are spontaneously created by people.

To avoid a possible misunderstanding I should say that there seems to me no difference in principle so far as *creativity* is concerned between *inventing* a new word (like 'valency' or 'biodegradable') and *learning* a word that is already in use, like 'bread' or 'left' and 'right'. Of course, inventing a new word may mark a breakthrough in physical chemistry or environmental studies, but leaving that aside, the use of any word, new or old, is creative in the sense that, say, having a fairly simple sensation is not creative. What you *see* is more or less determined by how the world is around you; what you *say* is not so determined. You may choose to speak of your world in an indefinite number of ways, only contingently limited by the vocabulary available to you. It is this capacity to conceptualize the world in an indefinite number of ways, and to construct an indefinite number of sentences, that lies at the root of human freedom. It is because, and to the extent that, we act not simply in terms of how we have to experience the world sensually, but in terms of how we *symbolize* it, that our activity is free. And this is the special and characteristic mark of human society. The fact that human communication involves the free and creative use of symbols, and the fact that human beings live together in political society, are two sides of the same truth. It is because of this that a whole range of words such as 'crime', 'commitment', 'conversation', 'exploitation', 'liberation', 'loyalty', 'tradition', 'drama' and 'revolution' are used literally in accounts of this human society, though we sometimes extend them metaphorically to other animal groupings or even more remote areas.

10

Son of God

What are we to make of the Christian tradition that Jesus was and is Son of God? Well, first of all, what are we *not* to make of it?

We will get absolutely nowhere if we compare it to stories about gods appearing in human form. But we might get somewhere if we start by contrasting it with them.

When Pallas Athena appears to Odysseus she is a goddess, normally resident on Olympus, who occasionally comes down to appear to him in human guise – or, more accurately, human *dis*guise. Jesus is not A god ι he is the God

1. [Now whatever else the church has been preaching for two thousand years, it is not that Jesus was a god, and not that he appeared guised or disguised as a human being, Jesus was one of us, a human being in a perfectly ordinary sense. So far as being human goes, the only difference between Jesus and me is that he lived out his humanity more consistently than I do.

I am occasionally tempted to pretend to myself that I am some kind of god. Jesus never for one moment had the illusion that he was a god. Pallas Athena belongs to myth – a perfectly respectable literary genre, largely about gods and such. Jesus belongs to our history, which is almost exclusively about sinners. Christianity comes from Jews; and they had hardly any use for myth because they had no use for gods. True, their attempts at historical writing were often as imaginative as, say, Shakespeare's *Richard III*. But they were not meant to be myths.

One important bit of history is the extraordinary effect that Jesus had on his followers after he had been killed. They were convinced that Jesus, whom they had lost in death, had returned to be present to them. They were also convinced that somehow because of this they had been filled with the spirit or breath or life of God himself.

The presence of Jesus after his death was not like being haunted by his ghost: it was almost exactly the opposite. For the culture of those who first came to believe in Jesus's return, you would be haunted by a ghost if you had failed to carry out the proper funeral rites for the dead – if, for example, the corpse was not properly buried. A ghost is a chilling reminder of death and the obligations it lays upon the living. This is not at all what Mary Magdalene and the others experienced, as the Gospel stories insist. What they encountered was the living Christ, present (and more present) than he had been before. They encountered not his ghost or his dismembered spirit, and certainly not just his memory (all of which would imply his actual absence), but himself as bodily present. Theologians dispute about the extent to which the stories of the appearances of Jesus narrate what brought about this conviction, and to what extent they are an expression of it. Common sense suggests a bit of each. Anyway, the conviction was powerfully there.

And what does this say about Jesus? There was a difference between what could be said about him before his death and what has to be said about him if you share the conviction of his followers. The first is accessible to all historians (and today's historians seem to find it rather more accessible than some Christian theologians used to think). Historians now know enough about the Jewish milieu of Jesus to be able to assert that he was a prophet and, in any ordinary sense, a saint – with only this little niggling worry: that he seemed to find himself more important than most saints would do. You see, once we have got rid of the ludicrous idea put about by quite a lot of Christians that the Pharisees and other Jewish contemporaries of Jesus hated him because they didn't believe in God's love and mercy and grace, but instead worshipped a set of regulations, once we have undemonized the enemies of Jesus, we have to look elsewhere to explain their hostility. And the most plausible answer seems to be that, while of course Jesus was in no way opposed to the Law, the Torah, God's own word of righteousness, he did seem to suggest that to follow him, even if you were wicked, was even more important than being devoted to the Law. So, understandably, some pious, educated Jews found him a subversive egotistical nuisance. There is no doubt that they did oppose him, and very little doubt that this was what gave Pontius Pilate an excuse to have him executed.

So: Jesus had the generosity, insight and courage of a saint – but maybe flawed by a streak of egotism. Or, again, maybe it was something else. I suppose that is as far as a historian could go. But after his death there were some Jews who were convinced that it *was* something else. Convinced that Jesus was not dead but once more humanly, which is to say *bodily*, alive (only more so), and that this bodily presence is the source of divine life for his followers, they said he was, in truth, more important than the Law because he was the fulfilment of the Torah, the embodiment of the righteousness of God.

The earliest Christians began to see Jesus not just as *preaching* the imminent coming of the divine kingship of love, but as *inaugurating* it in his own person. Not just a prophet and saint, but the source of the Spirit, the source of all prophecy and sanctity. Not just as one who received the Spirit, but one through whom the Spirit gave life to others; and not just to the community that had been blessed with the earlier revelation of God's love, the Jews, but even to those outside, to all the people of the world.

The phrase 'Son of God' had hitherto been a fairly normal way of describing a person or community that was sacred, set apart by God, or holy. But, by at least the time of Matthew, it had become not a general term to say what sort of person this is, but an answer to the question 'Who do you say that I am?', and Matthew has Peter saying: 'You are the Messiah [the

Spirit-bearer], the Son of the living God.' And Jesus responds: 'Blessed are you, Simon son of Jonah! For flesh and blood [we might paraphrase this as 'historical research'] has not revealed this to you, but my Father in heaven' (Mt. 16.16–17). A son of God is no longer *what* someone is; the Son of God is *who* Jesus is. And for Matthew, this conviction is the 'rock' upon which the church is founded (Mt. 16.18).

This church thought long and hard about what this meant. Already Matthew has Jesus saying, 'All things have been handed over to me by my Father; and no one knows the Son except the Father, and no one knows the Father except the Son and anyone to whom the Son chooses to reveal him' (Mt. 11.27; this sounds like something from John, but it's much earlier). Already the first generation of Christians saw in the person – not the doctrine, but the historical person of Jesus – the revelation of the Father.

4. 'Faith' was not just a matter of agreeing with what Jesus said – as you might agree or disagree with what Aristotle said. It was a matter of recognizing the personal life, death and resurrection of Jesus as showing us what we worship: not a god but the eternal explosion of love which is at once Father, Son and Spirit. Jesus is a revelation of the Father because he is the Son come amongst us, as one of us.

I am human in exactly the same way as my parents – but it was they who made me so. I didn't make them so. That is a distinction between us. Christians came to see that the Child of God is just as divine as God the Parent. But he is divine because of the Parent and not the other way round. And this is the only distinction between them. Of course he could not be truly divine, as his Father is, if he were a creature: and so an early creed says, 'begotten, *not* made'.

Now, with us, there is another distinction between me and my parents: I am a distinct, separate individual, having my own share in the same human nature. This kind of separation/distinction could have no place in the godhead, for God is one. God is the whole of Godness. And so the creed goes on: 'Begotten, not made, of one Being with the Father.' So, said the Christians, Jesus is the Son, the reproduction of the Father. Not an *image* of God, for that is just humankind – through which we express our idea of God. 'Who Jesus is' is God's idea of God. In Jesus it is not just that we have a clue to understanding God: in Jesus God understands himself; he is, as John was to put it, the Word of God. And not just the Word of God to us, but the Word of God to himself. In understanding his divine life the Father has unfathomable joy and delight, and this divine delight and joy is the Holy Spirit that is poured out upon us when the Word or Son of God is made flesh and dwells amongst us.

Christians saw the concrete historical life of Christ as bringing us into the Love which we worship. To be filled with the Spirit that comes to us from the Father through the Son is to be taken up to share in the eternal exchange of love we call the Trinity.

The early Christian poem quoted by Paul in Philippians (2.6–11) shows us in our history the eternal relations of Father and Son. The human obedience of the Son to his mission from the Father to be one of us, an obedience unto death, is rewarded in his being raised up and established in his kingdom, which is nothing but the outpouring of the Spirit amongst his fellow men and women. Of course the eternal love is enacted in our world in the crucifixion, in blood and torture and death, because that is the sort of world we have made of God's creation: a tragic world in which loving obedience and faithfulness mean suffering and persecution. If we have faith in Christ, as John warns us, the world will hate us, because we challenge the illusions and lies and cruelties by which the powers of this world are sustained. But the heart of the Gospel is that in this faith we are taken up into the eternity of love in which the Father says, 'This is my Son, the Beloved, with whom I am well pleased' (Mt. 3.17). That is why we speak of Jesus as Son of God and source of the Spirit.

11

Forgiveness

It is very odd that people should think that when we do good
God will reward us and when we do evil he will punish us. I
mean it is very odd that Christians should think this, that God
deals out to us what we deserve. It is not, I suppose, really odd
that other people should; I suppose it is the commonest way of
thinking of God, for God tends to be just a great projection into
the sky of our moral feelings, especially our guilt-feelings. But
I don't believe in God if that's what he is, and it is very odd
that any Christian should, since there is so much in the gospels
to tell us differently. You could say that the main theme of the
preaching of Jesus is that God isn't like that at all.

Take the famous parable of the prodigal son (Lk. 15.11–32).
In this, the younger son goes to a distant country far from his
father and squanders all his father's gifts in debauchery and
generally having a high old time. After a bit he sees himself for
what he is, so as to say, 'I am no longer worthy to be called your
son; treat me as one of your hired servants.' What his sin has
done is to alter his whole relationship with his father; instead
of being a son he now should be treated as one who gets his
wages, gets exactly what he deserves. But there are two things
here; there is the fact that this is what his sin has *done*, and
there is the fact that he *recognizes* this. To make sure you see
that this is the crucial point of the story, Luke has it repeated
twice. The vital thing is that the son has recognized his sin for
what it is: something that changes God into a paymaster, or a
judge. Sin is something that changes God into a projection of

our guilt, so that we don't see the real God at all; all we see is some kind of judge. God (the whole meaning and purpose and point of our existence) has become a condemnation of us. God has been turned into Satan, the accuser of man, the paymaster, the one who weighs our deeds and condemns us.

It is very odd that so much casual Christian thinking should be a worship of Satan, that we should think of the punitive satanic God as the only God available to the sinner. It is very odd that the view of God as seen from the church should ever be simply the view of God as seen from hell. For damnation must be just being fixed in this illusion, stuck for ever with the God of the Law, stuck for ever with the God provided by our sin.

It is the great characteristic of sinners that they do not know that they are sinners, that they refuse to accept and believe that they are sinners. On the contrary, they have found all the ways of justifying and excusing themselves. The whole conversation in hell consists of the damned telling each other how it is all a terrible mistake and they should not be there at all because they are righteous and virtuous. The desperate boredom of this must be the *pain* of hell, but the thing that *constitutes* hell is that God can't be seen. All that can be seen is this vengeful punitive god who is Satan.

The younger son in the story has escaped hell because he has seen his sin for what it is. He has recognized what it does to his vision of God: 'I am no longer worthy to be called your son; treat me like one of your hired servants' (Lk. 15.21). And, of course, as soon as he really accepts that he is a sinner, he ceases to be one; knowing that you have sinned *is* contrition or forgiveness, or whatever you like to call it. The rest of the story is not about the father *forgiving* his son, it is about the father *celebrating*, welcoming his son with joy and feasting. This is all the real God ever does, because God, the real God, is just helplessly and hopelessly in love with us. He is unconditionally in love with us.

His love for us doesn't depend on what we do or what we are like. He doesn't care whether we are sinners or not. It makes no difference to him. He is just waiting to welcome us with joy and love. Sin doesn't alter God's attitude to us; it alters our attitude to him, so that we change him from the God who is simply love and nothing else, into this punitive ogre, this Satan. Sin matters enormously to us if we are sinners; it doesn't matter at all to God. In a fairly literal sense he doesn't give a damn about our sin. It is we who give the damns. We damn ourselves because we would rather justify and excuse ourselves, and look on our self-flattering images of ourselves, than be taken out of ourselves by the infinite love of God. Contrition or forgiveness (remember that it is we who forgive ourselves) is almost the exact opposite of excusing ourselves. It is a matter of accusing ourselves – for now the sons of man (people, human beings) have power on earth to forgive sins, power to recognize sin for what it is and so abolish it. Contrition, or forgiveness, is self-knowledge, the terribly painful business of seeing ourselves as what and who we are: how mean, selfish, cruel and indifferent and infantile we are.

The younger son recognizes a truth: that his sin had made him into a wage-earner, one who gets his deserts. And in the simple recognition of that, his sin is no more. Contrast him with the elder son: 'I have been working like a slave for you, and I have never disobeyed your command' (Lk. 15.29). Even though he is law-abiding and not debauched like his brother, he has not seen God for what he is. He thinks of himself as a wage-earner. He thinks that he should collect his pay-packet from God and demand what he deserves. Jesus presents us here with the frightening possibility of the virtuous and carefully law-abiding man who, because he is concerned with himself, with his own merits and virtues, and what he thinks he deserves, cannot see God any more than the profligate (who at least has a good time).

The younger son was in some ways in a happier condition, for it was fairly easy for him to see himself as depraved, ungrateful and selfish. His sins were fairly easily recognizable as sins. The older brother is in a more subtle danger, and a greater one. God and his love were hidden from the younger one by the almost childlike pleasures of the flesh. God is hidden from the older one by pride, the speciality of Satan.

But of course it isn't really easy for either of them; in fact it is impossible for both of them. Once you have deluded yourself with sin, once you have shut yourself off from God (rather than letting yourself be destroyed by his love, destroyed and remade, crucified and raised from the dead), once you have hidden his love from you behind your protective barrier, your blindfold of self-flattery, there is nothing at all you can do about it.

It is by the power of God, by the love of God coming to him even while he was in sin, that the younger brother became able to see himself for what he is; and this is contrition, this is forgiveness.

Never be deluded into thinking that if you have contrition, if you are sorry for your sins, God will come and forgive you – that he will be touched by your appeal, change his mind about you and forgive you. Not a bit of it. God never changes his mind about you. He is simply in love with you. What he does again and again is change your mind about him. That is why you are sorry. That is what your forgiveness is. You are not forgiven because you confess your sin. You confess your sin, recognize yourself for what you are, because you are forgiven. When you come to confession, to make a ritual proclamation of your sin, to symbolize that you know what you are, you are not coming in order to have your sins forgiven. You don't come to confession in order to have your sins forgiven. You come to celebrate that your sins *are* forgiven. You come to put on the best robe and the ring on your finger and the sandals on your feet, and to get drunk out of your mind, because your blindfold and your blindness have gone, and you can see the love God has for you.

Being contrite, self-aware, about your sin is the same as believing in the love of God, smashing the punitive satanic god and having faith in the real God who is sheer unconditional love for you. You could say that it is your faith in God's undeviating love for you that lets you risk looking at your sins for what they are. It's OK, you can admit the truth about yourself. It doesn't matter: God loves you anyway. To admit your sins is to proclaim your faith in God's love for you personally. Telling your sins to the church in the sacrament of confession is just a form of the creed; you are saying, 'I am really like this and all the same God loves me, God doesn't care about my sins, he cares about me.' God is just infinite, unconditional, unalterable, eternal love – and his love is for me and for all sinful people. That is the single statement that we make in the creed.

12

Immaculate Conception

I suppose that for ordinary civilized and liberal people of our time one of the most repulsive dogmas by which the Catholic Church oppresses her people is the doctrine that innocent babies are somehow born in sin. The doctrine of original sin is thought of as primitive, irrational and deeply pessimistic. Quite a number of Christians themselves seem to have quietly dropped it, and many of the rest find it embarrassing. Depressing as this must be for traditional Catholics, we can perhaps at least take some comfort from the newly widespread belief in the Immaculate Conception. The Catholic Church modestly proposes that just two people, Jesus and his mother, were immaculately conceived: for the modern liberal world, the immaculately conceived runs into millions – indeed, everybody is immaculately conceived. The humbler, more cautious, but perhaps more realistic, view of the traditional Catholic is that that thrilling vision is not yet, but is somehow to be realized only after a great transformation in the future.

The Immaculate Conception means nothing but the irrelevance of original sin, so let's take a quick look at *that*.

First of all, original sin does not mean that babies are born sinners; it means that they are born into a human race, a human world already distorted by sin by rejection of God's friendship – not by their own sin, of course, but the sin of others before them. Through no fault of their own, human babies begin life in an emotionally maladjusted world and are handicapped in coping with the attacks that life will make on them – and, most importantly, lack the power of the Holy Spirit of divine love which is the *only* way of coping with the pressure of their situation.

In all this, Catholics do not differ much from other critics of liberal progressive optimism – Marxists, for example, and Freudians. All three of us think that it is not much use trying to tackle serious human problems piecemeal, as they occur; we need to go back to a root cause in the past. Marxists trace it to our origin in an inhuman and disabling economic order, and Freudians, if I understand them, to our origin in an inhuman and disabling family structure. Catholics have the more cheerful doctrine that it is due to sin, the inhuman and disabling sin of the world. More cheerful because we can and have been liberated from this inhumanity by forgiveness of sin: by the forgiveness that comes to us through the cross of Christ. More cheerful because while Freudians see our disablement as being only *ameliorated*, and only by long and expensive therapy, and Marxists by long and even more expensive revolution, for traditional Catholics (though they may also be Marxists and/or Freudians, and so may think both their techniques valuable in helping with the remaining leftover *effects* of original sin) the root cause *itself* has already been dealt with as a gift and for free. What is required of us is that we accept the gift of faith in the Healer and his saving passion and death. Then, although we may (and will) still suffer somewhat from these leftover effects of original sin for a while, in suffering and temptation and struggle in this intermediate life, we are destined to be totally liberated from sin in the future with our victory over death and sin by our sharing in Christ's resurrection, by our bodily assumption into heaven.

And God has given us a pledge of this future in the Mother of Jesus. She is the sign and sacrament of the coming destiny of our virgin mother the church, from whose immaculate womb we were reborn in baptism (as we sing in the Easter Vigil). The Mother of Jesus is, in scriptural terms, the sign of what God does in Christ for those he loves, the sign of what it will be to be fully redeemed. In the Mother of Jesus is the promise that when we are assumed bodily into our new life (a life that is to be not only at last a fully *human* life but also a sharing in the eternal life which is God himself), when this happens, our rebirth, begun in baptism, will come to fulfilment and we shall be indeed as though immaculately conceived – freed from sin as though it had never been. Not that our past life could be cancelled or forgotten, but that our past sinful deeds will come to be seen as God always saw them, through their forgiveness, as *felices culpae* – happy faults, as we call the sin of Adam, at the Easter Vigil, as themselves part of the whole mysterious story of grace by which God has brought us forgiven sinners to himself in Christ. It is this future glory of the human race that we celebrate during the season of Advent, when we look to the future coming of the Kingdom, as we thank God, make eucharist to God, for the coming Immaculate Conception and Assumption of our Virgin Mother Church, prefigured and promised in the Virgin Mother Mary.

13

Freedom

When St Luke wants to tell us about the first message of Jesus, the clue to all that is to follow, he has him come back from his apprenticeship with John the Baptist, and his struggle with temptation, back to his home in Nazareth, and there in the synagogue he preaches his first recorded sermon (Lk. 4.16–27). And what he does is proclaim the year of the Jubilee. He quotes a poem from the book of Isaiah, saying he has come to 'proclaim release to the captives..., to let the oppressed go free, to proclaim the year of the Lord's favour'.

The year of the Lord's favour (or grace) is not a vague pious metaphor but a quite definite thing which the poet found in that odd collection of fantasies and wishful thinking we call the book of Leviticus. Here it is laid down that in every fiftieth year everyone returns to his ancestral lands – no matter whom they have been sold to in the meantime; all the people enslaved for debt were set free; all debts and obligations were cancelled; there was a rebirth of society in which everyone starts all over again as people living in freedom (Lev. 25.8–55). This was the year of the Jubilee, which means the year of proclamation, literally of 'playing the trumpet'. What is trumpeted forth in this year is the good news, or gospel, of the freedom of the people of God. It was a society without slavery, with no more domination of the poor by the rich, a return to ancestral primitive pastoral life.

But, of course, this never actually happened. There never was anything like a Jubilee year in Israelite history – that's what I

163

meant by 'fantasy' and 'wishful thinking'. What it expressed was not the actual legal situation but what the people of God would be when they were really the people of God. They were to be a community living in freedom.

Now Jesus says in his first sermon that this is what he is all about; he is announcing the fulfilment of the dream. He is the trumpet announcing the Jubilee: 'Today this scripture has been fulfilled in your hearing' (Lk. 4.21).

Well, what is this Jubilee freedom? And how is it to be achieved? The first thing to see is that freedom here is thought of as involving a whole transformation of society – it is not a matter of freeing individual slaves but of a whole society without slaves. It is not a matter of helping some destitute individual but of no longer taking for granted that there have to be rich and poor. In other words, Jesus is appealing to a tradition that says: only in a certain kind of society, with a certain kind of relationship between people, can there be freedom. It is not that we have a certain sort of society because people are just naturally free. We need a certain sort of society for there to be free people.

Well, what sort of society? There are, of course, two views about this. There are those who think the kind of society in which there is freedom is one which keeps out of the way as much as possible. We are free from other people. Freedom is being left alone. On this view, we have to strike a balance between freedom and the claims of society: all that is communal, public, social is likely to be a hindrance to freedom – it is a regrettable necessity which we should tolerate only as much as we have to. Freedom, on this view, means freedom from social constraints. It means doing your own thing as far as that is practicable and putting up with social regulations when you have to.

This is a very different picture from the one we get in the Bible – both in the Old and the New Testaments. Here God's people are said to be free *because* they live under the Torah, the

Law. Left to themselves, without the Torah, people will look for gods to enslave themselves to. That great summary of the Law, the ten commandments, is a charter of liberation. It begins: I have brought you out of slavery, you shall have no gods, you shall not be enslaved by religion. And it goes on: you shall not be enslaved by each other, you must not even be enslaved by work – be sure you take a day off every week; you must not let the young and vigorous despise the aged and the sick, or let the powerful bully exploit the weak. It is if you live under this law, in this kind of society, that you will preserve the freedom I have given you. Otherwise you will throw it away. Freedom is not automatic. It cannot be taken for granted. It depends on how people relate to each other, what sort of community they have their lives in.

Jesus unquestionably believed this: he thought the whole point and purpose of the Law was, and always had been, to enshrine and maintain a certain way of living together which he called love. There is not the slightest evidence that Jesus ever *contrasted* the Law with love, or set up love as an alternative to the Law. What he taught was that you misunderstand the Law unless you see that it is given to preserve love and so liberates those who are oppressed, sets the captives free.

Now what is the connection between freedom and love? It is this: that we receive our freedom as a gift from our friends, that we receive ourselves at the hands of others. We can understand this best by thinking about gifts and gratitude, about saying 'Thank you' for presents. For I want to say that it is in the society characterized by giving and receiving free gifts, the society built upon friendship and love, that freedom is possible – and in no other circumstances. Let me try to explain why.

What exactly are you doing when you say 'Thank you'? You are saying, 'I think of you.' You have just been given, say, a pint or a pullover, and you are saying, 'I am not just glad to have this *thing*, I *think of you* in your giving. I see this object you have given me as a sign, a manifestation of your friendship. I recognize that in giving me this you are giving me yourself.' Every true gift is a gift of yourself, and every 'Thank you' is an acknowledgement of this. In the Christian church, when we recognize in the bread and wine the gift of Christ's own self we call it the 'eucharist', which is just 'Thank you' in Greek. We see Christ in this gift.

But what is it to give yourself? What are you giving when you give yourself? You are giving that most precious of gifts which is *nothing*, space: space in which someone can *be*. When you give yourself in your gifts you are making no demands. A free gift demands no return, puts your friend under no obligation. It leaves her or him free. It is the very source of freedom. Above all, this is true of that supreme kind of giving we call *forgiving*.

All other material creatures are hemmed around by other creatures, cabined and confined by the rest of the universe – even if they look as if they are in empty space. There is no such thing as nothing in nature. The last edge of one thing is the first edge of the next. Give or take a little indeterminacy, everything is the prisoner of everything else. All these things live by strict laws; there is no generosity or forgiveness with them. It is only human beings that have real space around them, empty space, elbow-room, space they can grow into, space where there is no obligation, determination or constraint. And this space is the gift of others. This space is given to us or forgiven to us by our friends, by those who love us, who do not impose their gifts upon us but give them freely by giving us themselves in their gifts – and so we say 'Thank you': *I think through this gift to you* and to the space you have given me.

You can see this vividly enough in those who have grown up without much friendship and love and forgiveness. You can see how unfree they are – hag-ridden by anxieties, compulsively justifying themselves instead of seeking forgiveness, or proving to themselves that they matter, that they are important, that they really exist, because nobody has given them the space in which to be themselves, to be spontaneous, repentant, careless and generous. They have to be secure by gathering wealth or power and they are filled with terror if they cannot do this. And need I say that to some extent this is everybody's problem? It is not the love of money that is the root of all evil. The root of all evil is not being loved, or not recognizing that you are loved.

Yet Christians think that, however you are neglected and unloved by those around you, you are always in fact loved; God is for Christians nothing but the unconditional everlasting love that sustains us in being, and it is failure to recognize this love – as Christians would say, a lack of faith in this love – that is the root of evil. Unfortunately this lack of faith can go quite well with paid-up membership of the Christians' churches – just as faith can be seen in people who would be quite shocked to be accused of believing in God.

It is this awareness of being ultimately loved by God that makes freedom possible at all. But we find this love of God in the love we share with each other. That is why Jesus has two commandments: first the love we exchange with God, and then the love we exchange with each other.

So freedom depends on gratitude, on eucharist. Freedom depends first on being grateful for the space to exist, in which you *can* exist, for life, for being at all. We may have very little notion of who it is we are to be grateful to. Indeed, I think with the great philosopher St Thomas Aquinas that we have no idea at all what God is. St Thomas thought 'God' was just a label we use for whatever makes sense of our gratitude for existing. God is whatever we say 'Thank you' to. But then the exercise of our freedom depends on living in a society based on friendship, which is a society based on free giving and receiving. Those who are lucky find this to some extent in their families, but such families can only exist and survive if the same free giving is also the basis of the whole society in which they exist. Friendship, generosity, giving without demanding return, is not a luxury; it is not something for your spare time or your spare cash. It is the only atmosphere in which freedom can breathe.

In our world 'justice' has come to mean simply fairness, paying what you owe, fulfilling your obligations, obeying the law. And this is an excellent thing. But it is not a fundamental thing. When the Bible speaks of justice, *tsedech* or *dikaiosune*, it means first the generosity of God, the righteousness of God: the generosity conveyed to us in the Son of God, who was ready to be killed for the sake of sharing fully in our humanity, a generosity in which we have been allowed and called to share, so that we can live with each other not just by fairness and strict obligation but by friendship, so that we give each other space to be, so that we can live in what Paul calls 'the freedom of the glory of the children of God' (Rom. 8.21).

Index

metaphysics of contingency, the
64
miracles 101
morality 92–3, 107
Mother of Christ 161–2

Natural Theology (Paley) 75n.8
natural units 128–9
natural/unnatural behaviour
49–52, 54
non-contingent/contingent
things 63–5, 77
nothing 65, 118

omne agens agit sibi simile 58
omnipotence 68–9, 71–3, 76, 78,
93
origin of species 116, 118
Our Lady of Fatima 38

Paley, William 75
Pallas Athena 150
Paul, St 154, 168
perfection 114, 119
Peter, St 152
physics 109, 116
Pilate, Pontius 152
Plato 114
possibili et necessario 64
predestination 71
prodigal son, the 155–8
proof 31

quasi-units 128–9

reason 31
resurrection, the 7–8, 10, 29,
102
Roman Catholicism 22, 67, 160,
161

sacramental rites 36
St Paul 100
St Peter 120, 121–2
salvation 97
Satan 156–8
scientia media 72
self-movers 126–7, 130
selfishness 107
Shakespeare, William 44
sheep/wolf (example) 139,
145–7
significance 145–6
sin
and enjoyment 108
and evil 68, 71, 92
and God 82
and guilt 155–6, 158
and the love of God 97, 99,
158–9
origin of 38
original 160
and uncertainty 39
in the world 161–2
society 105–6
Socrates 46
soul, the 123, 132–3, 135
spirituality 139, 153, 154
stars 109–10, 118
state, the 39
Summa Theologiae (Aquinas) 63,
95–6n, 125n
sun, the 116
supernatural 21, 23, 27
symbols 141, 144, 149

*Teaching of the Catholic Church,
The* (McCabe) 124
ten commandments, the 46,
102–3, 165
Thatcher, Margaret 105

INDEX

CPSIA information can be obtained
at www.ICGtesting.com
Printed in the USA
LVHW080042200822
726389LV00007B/373